Riti

a Worshipping Heart

by

Dr.Muhammad Musa Ash-Shareef

Translated by

Abu Naasir Ibrahim Abdur-Rauf

Published by:

Dakwah Corner Bookstore (M) Sdn. Bhd.
No. 7, Jalan Dato Abdul Aziz, Section 14,
46100 Petaling Jaya, Selangor Darul Ehsan,
MALAYSIA
T: +603-7956 4664

DAKWAH CORNER BOOKSTORE

2nd Edition Published:
2020

Title:
Rituals of a Worshipping Heart

Author:
Muhammad Musa Ash-Shareef

Translator:
Abu Naasir Ibrahim Abdur-Rauf

ISBN:
978-983-4462-64-2

Director:
Farid Ullah Ahmed Hussain

Cover Design:
Mohammed Faraz

Typesetting:
Every Edition Sdn. Bhd.

Printed by:
Percetakan Azman Sdn. Bhd.

For suggestions and comments:
dakwahcornerpublications@gmail.com

Showroom Outlets

MALAYSIA

Dakwah Corner Bookstore
Ampang Point Shopping Centre
Tel: +603- 4266 9692

Dakwah Corner Bookstore
G15 (Ground Floor)
Amcorp Mall, Petaling Jaya
Tel: +60 3 7932 0079

SAUDI ARABIA

Dawah Corner Bookstore
Makkah Commercial Center, Holy Makkah
Tel: +966 125311 895

NIGERIA

Dawah Islamic Bookshop
UAC Building , Abuja
Tel: +234 805 603 7779

PHILIPPINES

Dakwah Corner Bookstore
Falcatan Street, Tetuan, Zamboanga City
Tel: +63 926 5384

Distributors

Darussalam Australia
Australia
Tel: +61 2 9740 7188

Salaam Media International
Singapore
Tel: +65 63964121

Darussalam Publishers
USA
Tel: +1 860 224 2400

Darussalam Books
(London Central Mosque), UK
Tel: +44 2077231234

Contents

PART 2

Some Basic Heart-Related Worship

Introduction

All praise is due to Allah who taught with the pen. He favoured us tremendously and saved us from wrath, ignorance and disbelief. He made us to be from the *Ummah* of the best of creatures, Muhammad ﷺ (May Allah send blessings and peace upon him) and by that, He favoured us over all creation and raised us, through that blessed affiliation, over the entire jinns and men.

So, it behooves us to regularly praise Allah (the Exalted), with glorification and sanctification, and be from His sincere soldiers, who are saved from the deceptions of uncertainty and despair until we will be favoured on the Plane of Resurrection, secured, and be shaded from the shade of the Throne of the Most-Merciful. We will be called, 'You are servants of Allah and His saved party, from those who are not to fear or grief. Enter into Paradise and take delight with the Look at the Sublime Face, and safe from the awful, whether major or minor.

Enjoy the company of the prophets, the truthful ones, the martyrs, the pious ones, the service of the *hoor* and the benefiting young boys. The angels will visit you from every door (saying): 'Peace be upon you. What an excellent blissful end and resort! What a great sight, noble image, lofty enjoyment, and tremendous blessing!' May Allah make you and me to be from those who will be adorned with it from His Power, Might and Generosity.

To proceed:

The pious predecessors ﷺ (may Allah be pleased with them) excelled in understanding of the cure of the hearts and made it stick to servitude to Allah with delight and crave. They cured it of its inadequacies and defects and their hearts were virtuous like their deeds and pure like their intentions. So, Allah (the Exalted) ordained acceptance for them with the angels and men, saved them from restlessness and the evils of the whisperings of the one who withdraws. He raised their ranks as rewards for their heart-related efforts, made them believers and chose them with knowledge over all creatures.

Since we are commanded to follow their pure path; their blessed acts of worship and righteous deeds, I intend to explain their attitude towards their hearts and the importance of making the hearts turn to its Lord. I have also established a comparison between the heart-related acts of worship and those of the limbs intending by all of that, the purification of our souls so that its hardness is eased off and the sin that has put it in disorder and disobedience is cleared.

We ask Allah to purify our hearts and make it steadfast out of His Greatness. May He grant this to us all. All praise is due to Allah, the Lord of the Worlds.

Dr. Muhammad Musa Ash-Shareef

Publisher's Note

Dr. Muhammad Musa Shareef is considered from among the few who combined remarkable excellence in many fields of study. In addition to being a pilot in command of a commercial airliner, he obtained a doctorate in the Qur'an and *Sunnah* and memorized the Qur'an with certification from Shaykh Ayman Suwayd.

Piety, submissiveness and devoutness, love, pleasure, fear and hope are from the heart-related acts of worship which indicate the servant's belief in his Lord, (the Exalted), show its strength, bring rest to the mind and shower on it, the coldness of tranquillity. It fills the soul of the true servant with the love of Allah, the Mighty and Sublime, and by it, the servant attains sincere servitude to Allah (the Exalted).

Thus, the book you hold, honourable reader, contains the humble presentation of matters related to the Heart's worship and its impact in the life of the Muslim. So, we present to you, an English translation of the book beseeching Allah (the Exalted), to grant us benefit by it and reward the author with abundant good for He Alone, grants success.

Farid Ullah Bin Ahmed Hussain
Kuala Lumpur

PART 1

The Heart and its Worship

Preamble

The Status of the Heart's Worship from the *Salaf*

The Meaning of Salaf: It is said, 'the thing *sa-la-fa*' to mean that, 'it went past', and so-and-so *sa-la-fa*: come or go before (something or people).

And *As-Salaf*: is every pious act put forward. It is also every person who has gone past from the fathers, grandfathers and near relatives who have gone past in age (i.e. older) and honour. Thus, the first generation amongst the *Tabi'un* (the students of the companions), were referred to as *As-Salaf As-Saalih* (the Pious Predecessors).[1]

Some have limited the (word) *Salaf* to refer to the first three generations based on the saying of the Prophet ﷺ: "The best of my community are those in my time, then those who follow them and then, those who follow them…"[2] And anyone who follows the methodology of the *Salaf* and takes after them to this present time is from them.

People have been kept seriously occupied with following the sayings of the *Salaf* related to *'Aqeedah* (creed) and *Fiqh*

1 *Taajul-'Urs*: *sa-la-fa*

2 Reported by Al-Bukhaari in his *Sahih*: The Book of The Virtues of the Companions of the Prophet ﷺ and the One who accompanied the Prophet ﷺ or saw him Amongst the Muslims is From his Companions.

(Jurisprudence), and they have excelled in understanding all that.[3] However, only slight attention is given to the righteous acts of the predecessors; the strength of their *Iman*, the greatness of their *Yaqeen* (certainty of faith) and the condition of their hearts.[4]

So, the hearts in people – except whomever Allah shows mercy – got corrupted and their eyes became empty. They are not been influenced by admonitions, not abstaining from prohibitions and are not acting upon good deeds except only littly.

The one who studies the biography of the Prophet ﷺ in Madeenah - after the people had entered into Islam and the religion became established – will realize that the issues of *'Aqeedah* (creed) were few when compared with admonition, stories, etiquettes, remembrance of Allah and character. The Prophet ﷺ only gave great attention to *'Aqeedah* at the

3 The emphasis placed on the teaching of the *'Aqeedah* and *Fiqh* of the pious predecessors as the basis for the Muslim is based on many verses of the Qur'aan and authentic narrations from Allah's Messenger ﷺ and many statements reported from the pious predecessors. Imam Ibn Qayyim Al-Jawziyyah رحمه الله explains saying: "Whoever desires high elevation of his building then he has to fortify its foundations and follow its proper dimensions. So, the actions (the various acts of worship) and ranks (desired from the worship) are the building and its foundation is the *Iman*. Therefore, the major interest of the learned is the perfection of the foundation and dimensions but the ignorant raises the structure without foundation and his structure collapses as soon as it is erected. See: *Sittu Durar min Usooli Ahl il-Athar* pg. 16. **(TN)**

4 The invitation to *Tasfiyah wat-Tarbiyah* (Rectification and Education) is one that is all-encompassing including the *Aqeedah* and the *Fiqh* related matters both of which contain the heart-related acts of worship. It has included the manners of learning and all other details of the religion. Lots of the teachings and writings of the scholars - past and present, is evidence for this. Thus, these scholars and their students, generation after generation, have not only taught the creed and character, they have – Allah willing, been epitomes of righteousness. On the other hand, when the people do not understand the substance of the matters of creed and *Fiqh* the consciousness required to agitate other sincere heart-related acts of worship and enviable characters become missing! **(TN)**

beginning of his call to the non-Muslims in Makkah. Later on when the people entered the religion and the nation became formed in Madeenah, he began to nurture the souls with *Jihad*, admonitions and manners. He would only give reminders on the matters of *'Aqeedah* when the need arose as it happened with the companions about the tree they saw at Hunayn.

Abu Waaqid Al-Laythy ﷺ (may Allah be pleased with him) said that: They left from Makkah with Allah's Messenger ﷺ to Hunayn. He said: "The idolaters used to have a lote tree where they used to stay and hang their weapons, called, *Dhaat Anwaat*."[5] He continued, "So we passed by a huge, green, lote tree and said, 'O Allah's Messenger, get us a *Dhaat Anwaat* – and in another version - as the idolaters have *Dhaat Anwaat*. So, the Messenger of Allah ﷺ said: 'I swear by the One in whose Hand is my soul! You have spoken as the people of Musa did:

.... ٱجْعَل لَّنَآ إِلَٰهًا كَمَا لَهُمْ ءَالِهَةٌ ۚ قَالَ إِنَّكُمْ قَوْمٌ تَجْهَلُونَ ﴿١٣٨﴾

«'Make for us a god as they have gods.' He said: 'Verily, you are a people who know not (the Majesty and Greatness of Allah and what is obligatory upon you'».

Al-A'raf (Q7:138)

They are paths. You shall follow the paths of those before you, a practice after the other." In another wording, the

5 The name a particular tree which belonged to the idolaters; they used to hang their weapons on it to seek good omen. See 'Fath ur-Rabbaanee' 1/199.

Prophet ﷺ then said: "*Allahu Akbar* (Allah is the Greatest), this was as the Children of Israel said to Musa…"[6]

And as the Prophet ﷺ taught the man who said: "As Allah wills and you will". He ﷺ said to him: "Do you make me *'Idlan* (equal)[7] with Allah? Rather, (say): As Allah, alone wills!"

Similarly, the Prophet ﷺ said to the companions: "You were making a statement regarding which shyness for you had prevented me from prohibiting you from it." He said: "Do not say, 'As Allah wills and as Muhammad wills'". He ﷺ also said to them: "You should say; 'As Allah wills and then Muhammad'".[8]

The Prophet ﷺ also taught the Bedouin who said, "O Messenger of Allah! The mind is overstrained, the household is lost, the possessions have lessened,[9] and the livestock is destroyed. Ask Allah to grant us rain. We intercede with Allah by you and with you by Allah." The Messenger of Allah ﷺ retorted, "Woe unto you! Do you know what you are saying?" The Messenger of Allah ﷺ said the *Tasbeeh* (*subhaanAllah* – meaning – Glorious is Allah) and continued to say the *Tasbeeh* until change was seen in the countenance of the companions.[10] Thereafter, he said: "Woe unto you! Certainly, intercession is not sought by Allah with any one

---

6 Reported by Imam Ahmad رحمه الله. See the last reference; Shaykh Ahmad Abdur-Rahmaan Al-Banna رحمه الله had mentioned that the chain of the Hadith is *Jayyid* (good).

7 i.e. a partner and like: see 'the last reference' (1/38).

8 Imam Ahmad رحمه الله has reported all of these wordings and others, and the chains of these wordings are *Jayyid* (good). See the last reference.

9 i.e. reduced: See 'Awn ul-Ma'bud' (13/12)

10 i.e. the signs of the change in his noble face was noticed on the faces of his companions because they understood from his repetition of the *Tasbeeh* that he became annoyed from that and they feared his annoyance.

among His creatures. Allah is far above. Woe to you! Do you know Who Allah is...?"[11]

It becomes necessary in that case, that this is what the Muslims should do today. Since many of them have the right *'Aqeedah*,[12] it will be necessary to call attention to *'Aqeedah*-related errors only when such occurs and then go on with the admonitions, reminders, *Jihad*, *Iman* and character-related training.

However, the one who studies the condition of the society - which is geared towards abstract matters that most of its people do not understand and is denied correct education and following the Book of Allah, the *Sunnah* of His Messenger ﷺ and the way of the Pious Predecessors رضي الله عنهم - will wonder why it fails regarding commandments and engages in forbidden things? It gets accustomed to sinfulness, trivializing the major sins and acting upon them.

This is because abstract matters only benefit the people of knowledge and its students. As for the rest of the community, they only become obedient with matters other than these. The biography of the Prophet ﷺ is with us and it makes it clear that his methodology with which he nurtured the companions in Madeenah is the methodology that is preferred for education until the Last Day. And Allah knows best.

But if the benefit is related to the unbelievers or the people of misguided beliefs, then the methodology of the Prophet ﷺ in Makkah is the right approach that should be employed

---

11 Reported by Imam Abu Dawud in his *Sunan*, 'The Book of the *Sunnah*', Chapter on the *Jahmiyyah*; and the Hadith is *Hasan* (good) – Allah willing – and there is an extensive discussion on it. See the last reference (13/11-35)

12 Given proper consideration, it is obvious that this conclusion is away from the reality on the ground. **(TN)**

with them since most of his sayings there, were regarding *Tawheed* (the Oneness of Allah).[13]

As for *Al-'Ibaadah*, it is an all-encompassing noun for all what Allah loves and is pleased with of sayings and actions, both secret or open.[14]

So, when I speak about the heart-related acts of worship, I only mean the secret actions which influence the open actions of the limbs and statements.

13 Given proper consideration again, it is obvious that this conclusion really lacks evidence – and in fact contradicts other clear evidences from the Qur'aan and Hadith and the ways of the pious predecessors. **(TN)**

14 It is the definition of *Shaykh ul-Islaam* Ibn Taimiyyah ﷺ and it a widely known definition. See: *Tayseer ul-'Azeez il-Hameed* pg. 46.

Chapter 1
The Meaning of *Qalb*

What is intended in this section is to specify the limb which is responsible for perception and cognitive response: Is it the heart in the chest or the brain?

As for the *Qalb* (heart), it has two meanings in Arabic: "One of the two (meanings) points to the pure aspect of something and its virtuous part, while the other points to returning a thing from one side to the other.

1.1 The First Meaning

The first meaning is to do with the heart of man and others. It is so named because it is the most virtuous and most uplifted thing in him. The most pure aspect of a thing and the most virtuous of all things is its heart."[15] The first definition is intended in this section.

The *Qalb* (the heart) was so named for its turning over and over:

The *Qalb* is not so named, except for its turning over and

15 *Mu'jam Maqaayeesil-Luggah*: *Qalb*.

over. But the *Ra'y* (intellect) changes with man, stage after stage.[16]

There are many statements concerning the *Qalb* in the Book of Allah the Mighty and Sublime and the narrations from Allah's Messenger ﷺ. However, does it refer to that limb that exists in the chest or the intellect in the brain? Views have varied on this matter.

Nevertheless my view regarding it – and Allah knows best – is that the *Qalb* is neither his nor that. It is rather "a worship-inclined nature which has a strong connection with the bodily heart."[17] It is also connected to the brain and its sensual and nervous inkling to a level known only to Allah the Mighty and Sublime.

I have held this view by way of reconciling what has been reported in the verses of the Qur'aan and the Hadith which may refer to the physical heart in the chest and the sayings of some of the scholars of *Tafseer* and others amongst those who view that what is intended by the *Qalb* in the verses is the intellect in the brain. A group of the experts in anatomy today also hold this view.

I will first state the noble verses from which it is understood that what is intended by the *Qalb* is the physical heart within the ribs, and thereafter mention the view of those who opine that it refers to the intellect in the brain.

Firstly: The verses and Hadith that show that the *Qalb* is the physical heart in the chest. I will cite the texts depending on their clarity and also start with the *Ahadith* with strong

16 *Lisaanul-'Arab*: *Qa-Laam-Baa*.

17 *At-Ta'reefaat*: *Qalb*, and this good-nature does not necessarily imply that it cannot be seen or that it is abstract and not physical. Rather, it could be present in reality and yet, the person does not discover it; and Allah knows best.

denotation on this subject. They are even almost clear-cut texts on it:

1. Anas bin Maalik رضي الله عنه said, "Jibreel (*alayh as-Salaam*) came to Allah's Messenger ﷺ while he was playing with some children. He took him, brought him to the ground and opened his chest. He took out the *Qalb* and removed a flesh from it. He then said: 'This is the lot of *Shaytaan* in you'. He washed it in a golden container with Zam-zam water. Then he closed it up and returned it to its place." Anas رضي الله عنه said regarding it: "I used to see the sign of that stitching on his chest."[18] This statement from Anas رضي الله عنه is clear that the *Qalb* refers to the heart within the chest.

   A number of the scholars of *Tafseer* have mentioned this story in the explanation of His saying:

أَلَمْ نَشْرَحْ لَكَ صَدْرَكَ ۝١

«Have We not opened your breast for you (O Muhammad (Peace be upon him))?"

Ash-Sharh (Q94:1)

The actions of Jibreel (*alayh as-salaam*) with the Prophet's *Qalb* indicate that the physical *Qalb* in the human body has a flesh or (a good-nature) which influences the actions of man. This flesh may be physical or abstract. If it is physical, it could be extremely small and invisible to the naked-eyes – And Allah knows Best. Yet, modern medical practice has not discovered the qualities of

18 Reported by Imam Muslim in his *Sahih*: the Book of *Iman*: Chapter of the Journey (to *Masjidul-'Aqsa*) with the Messenger ﷺ : 2/362-363

this flesh; and non-discovery is not evidence of non-existence.

2. The Prophet ﷺ said: "Certainly, the body has a morsel of flesh; when it is upright, all of the body is upright. And when it is corrupted; all of the body is corrupted and that is the heart".[19]

   The Prophet's ﷺ saying, "a morsel of flesh" is a clear text regarding the physical *Qalb* in the human body. It refutes interpretation of *Majaaz* on it. And he ﷺ does not speak of his own desire it is only an inspiration he is given.

   Ibn Hajar[20] رحمه الله said, "This is used as evidence that the intellect is in the *Qalb* (heart)."[21]

3. The Hadith of the Prophet ﷺ about fearing Allah and his pointing to his chest. Abu Hurayrah رضي الله عنه said, Allah's Messenger ﷺ said, "Do not be envious of one another... Piety is in this place" – and he pointed to his chest three times – "[22]

4. Allah the Mighty and Sublime said:

---

19 Reported by Imam Al-Bukhaari: The Book of *Iman*: Chapter of the One who Exonerated Himself for His Religion: 1/2

20 He is Shaykh ul-Islam Ahmad bin 'Ali bin Muhammad, the leader of the scholars of Hadith in his time. He was born in Egypt in the year 773 AH and he made great efforts in the various sciences until he reached the peak. He was given appointments. He died in the year 852 AH at Cairo. See his biography in *Ad-Dao ul-Laami'*: 2/36-40

21 *Fath ul-Baaree*: 1/211

22 Reported by Imam Muslim in his *Sahih*: The Book of Benevolence, Relationship and Etiquettes: Chapter on Prohibition of Wronging the Muslim, Disgracing him and Scorning him: 16/93,94

.... فَإِنَّهَا لَا تَعۡمَى ٱلۡأَبۡصَٰرُ وَلَٰكِن تَعۡمَى ٱلۡقُلُوبُ ٱلَّتِي فِي ٱلصُّدُورِ ﴿٤٦﴾

«Verily, it is not the eyes that grow blind, but it is the hearts which are in the breasts that grow blind.»

Al-Hajj (Q22:46)

So, His saying the Exalted: **"which are in the breasts"** contradicts any *Majaaz.*[23] However, it could be the abstract *Qalb* although the statement could refer to the actual one (i.e. the heart).

5. Allah the Exalted said:

أَفَلَمۡ يَسِيرُواْ فِي ٱلۡأَرۡضِ فَتَكُونَ لَهُمۡ قُلُوبٞ يَعۡقِلُونَ .... ﴿٤٦﴾

«Have they not travelled through the land, and have they hearts wherewith to understand».

Al-Hajj (Q22:46)

He the Mighty and Sublime did not say, "intellect wherewith to understand" - for example - despite its congruence with the text.

It will be understood from these evidences that what is intended by the *Qalb* is the heart in the human body and its covert connection with the actions and intentions of man.

Secondly: From the things that necessitated my viewpoint is that modern medicine does not know till date – certainly and absolutely – what actually (physically, in the human

23 *Majaaz*: the use of a word for other than what it was originally set.

body) influences the abstract actions and intentions of man? Where is the place of perception and abstract sensation? It only recognizes what influences (in the human body), the physical actions, which is the brain. In that case, it would imply that the heart has some attributes not discovered till date; and the verses and *Ahadith* I stated earlier, will help on this possibility.

Thirdly: The joint influence of the intellect and the heart. The viewpoint is further strengthened by the fact that since man's physical existence is apparently connected to the heart and intellect together, then his intending and sensing could also be connected with the heart and intellect together. This is because man cannot exist normally except that his heart and intellect are sound. So, why shouldn't there be between his heart and intellect, a strong connection which will influence his abstract actions or what we call the Heart's worship, its sicknesses and his sensations and internal perceptions?

This link is still not known just as the reality of sleep is still obscure and as the essence of vision is yet unknown – And Allah knows Best.

Fourthly: This viewpoint will harmonize between those who opine that the intellect is in the heart and that it has no link with the brain, and those who view that the intellect is in the brain and that it has no connection with the heart.

Imam An-Nawawi[24] رحمه الله summarized these explanations while commenting on the Hadith, "Certainly, the body has a morsel of flesh". He said: "This Hadith is cited as evidence that the intellect is in the heart and not in the head, and there is a widely known difference on it. The position of

24 He is the great Imam, the ascetic Yahya bin Sharaf bin Mura Ash-Shafi'i, the great scholar of Hadith and jurist. He died in Nawa in Shaam (Ancient Syria) in the year 676 AH. See his biography in *Fawaat al-Wafayaat*: 4/264-268.

our teachers and the majority of the people of scholastic theology is that it is in the heart. But Abu Hanifa said that it is in the brain, or as may also be said, the head. The first opinion is also reported of the philosophers and the second, of the medical doctors…"

Then, Imam An-Nawawi mentioned some of the evidences of those who view that the intellect is in the heart – as I stated earlier – and then said, "Those who view that it is in the brain cite as evidence, that if the brain is corrupted, the intellect becomes corrupted and – in their view – there will be collapse due to the corruption of the brain. This does not contain evidence for them because Allah (the Exalted) has made it common that when the brain is corrupted, the intellect also becomes corruption even though the intellect is not inside it and there is no denying this…"[25]

Shaykh al-Islam Ibn Taimiyyah رحمه الله said: "It is said that the intellect is in the brain – according to many of the medical doctors – and is quoted from Imam Ahmad. But some of his students (and those who follow them) view that: the foundation of the intellect is in the heart and that when it becomes perfect, it gets to the brain. However, the source of thought and reflection is the brain while the source of intention is the heart. The intellect could be taken to mean knowledge or deed; and the initiation of knowledge and willful deed is wish and the initiation of the wish is in the heart. The one who intends a thing cannot be so called until he conceives the intended. So, the heart must be conceiving so that this and that comes from it."[26] The saying of Ibn Taimiyyah will be considered a supporting proof in this case.

25 See: *Sharh Sahih Muslim* (11/209)

26 *Majmoo' Fataawah*: 9/303, and I have quoted that from the book: *Al-Qalb wa Wazaaifuhu fil Kitaab was-Sunnah*.

Imam Ibn Katheer[27] رحمه الله said in the explanation of His saying:

وَجَعَلَ لَكُمُ السَّمْعَ وَالأَبْصَارَ وَالأَفْئِدَةَ

«And He gave you hearing, sight, and hearts.»

An-Nahl (Q16:1)

"The *Af-idah* are the intellects whose foci - based on the authentic position - are the hearts. It is also said to be the brain."[28]

Then, it is appropriate to say - in harmonizing and reconciling what is understood from the noble verses, the *Ahadith* and the statements of the leading scholars and experts in Anatomy, that: the *Qalb* has strong connections with perceptions, sensations and responses and that occurs in a manner known only to Allah (the Exalted). And that the heart also has links in manners unknown to the scientists of the present day; and that what links the heart and intellect is also not known till date.

I have only said that because the intellect has abstract duties which cannot be denied and it is necessary to harmonize

27 He is Ismaa'eel bin Umar bin Katheer, from Basra, the Shaafi'ee scholar, Imaad ud-Deen. He was born in the year 700 AH and he grew up in Dimash (Ancient Syria) and he died there in the year 774 AH after he went blind at the before his death. He has noble works and was a scholar of Hadith. See his biography in: *Ad-Duraa Al-Kaaminah:* 1/399-400.

28 *Tafseer ul-Qur'aan il-'Azeem*: 4/508

between the view that it influences and that the heart also influences simultaneously – And Allah knows Best.[29]

29 There are a number of occurrences – which are not confirmed scientifically, to my knowledge – which speaks of change in some human innate dispositions due to the transplant of the heart of others to it. It is said that there were changes in the innate dispositions of one of those who got the pig heart transplant done for him. If this is true scientifically, it will be a proof that strengthens what I had mentioned earlier.
There is a matter that requires some precise scientific explanation, and that is: the increase in the heart beats during the perceptions of fear, or emotional changes and others; is it purely an action of the brain which causes stimulation in the heart or it is a combined action of the heart and the brain? This matter requires precise scientific explanations and I do not know if the medical scientists have facts regarding this issue or not.

Chapter 2

Virtues and Importance of the Heart

The heart has many virtues, several peculiarities and profound importance when compared to other limbs such as:

1. It is Humbled by Divine Will and Intervention

The texts of the *Sharee'ah* are full of showing the Heart's honour, its importance and the greatness of its influences. They also contain explanations that Allah (the Exalted) does what He likes with the hearts of man. Thus, Allah comes in between a person and his heart:

وَٱعۡلَمُوٓاْ أَنَّ ٱللَّهَ يَحُولُ بَيۡنَ ٱلۡمَرۡءِ وَقَلۡبِهِۦ وَأَنَّهُۥٓ إِلَيۡهِ تُحۡشَرُونَ ﴿٢٤﴾

«And know that Allah comes in between a person and his heart».

Al-Anfal (Q8:24)

Also, Allah the Mighty and Sublime makes the hearts of the believers strong and firm and so, they are patient:

وَرَبَطْنَا عَلَىٰ قُلُوبِهِمْ إِذْ قَامُوا۟ فَقَالُوا۟ رَبُّنَا رَبُّ ٱلسَّمَٰوَٰتِ وَٱلْأَرْضِ .... ﴿١٤﴾

«And We made their hearts firm and strong when they stood up and said: «Our Lord is the Lord of the heavens and the earth.»

Al-Kahf (Q18:14)

Likewise Allah casts terror in the hearts of the enemies:

.... وَقَذَفَ فِي قُلُوبِهِمُ ٱلرُّعْبَ .... ﴿٢﴾

«And He cast terror into their hearts…»

Al-Hashr (Q59:2)

These references and others evince the virtue of the heart and its great importance.

2. It has Legal Responsibility

Since *Islam*, *Iman* and *Ihsan* and what comes after them from the inward acts of worship have their place is the heart, then the heart is where Allah (the Exalted) looks at. The Prophet ﷺ said, "Allah does not consider your bodies or your looks but He looks at your hearts" – and he pointed at his noble chest.[30]

3. The Rightly-Guided Heart is Greatly Sufficed

The rightly guided-heart has light and insight that Allah grants whom He wills among His slaves. Through it, He protects him from various harms and guides him to abundant goodness such as *Al-Ilhaam*.[31] Allah (the Exalted) says:

وَأَوْحَيْنَآ إِلَىٰٓ أُمِّ مُوسَىٰٓ أَنْ أَرْضِعِيهِ ۖ فَإِذَا خِفْتِ عَلَيْهِ فَأَلْقِيهِ فِى ٱلْيَمِّ وَلَا تَخَافِى
وَلَا تَحْزَنِىٓ ۖ إِنَّا رَآدُّوهُ إِلَيْكِ وَجَاعِلُوهُ مِنَ ٱلْمُرْسَلِينَ ﴿٧﴾

---

30 Reported by Imam Muslim in his *Sahih*: The Book of Benevolence, Relationship and Etiquettes: Chapter on Prohibition of Wronging the Muslim, Disgracing him and Scorning him: 16/94. **TN:** "And Imam Muslim and others have reported an increment: **'...and your actions'**. This increment is very important because many people wrongly understand this Hadith without it. So, when you enjoin them what the noble *Sharee'ah* has commanded them like leaving the beard, abstaining from imitating the non-Muslims (in acts that are specifically known with them) and things like that from the obligations of the *Sharee'ah*, they say to you that the main thing is what is in the heart and they make evidence – in their view – with this Hadith, not knowing this authentic increment that proves that Allah – Blessed is He and the most High – also looks at their actions. So, if it is righteous, He accepts it and if not, then he rejects it as is pointed to by many texts like his saying – ﷺ – 'Whoever invents into this matter what is not from it; it shall be rejected'. And the truth is that it is not possible to imagine the rightness of the heart except with the rightness of the actions or the rightness of the actions except with the rightness of the hearts; and Allah's Messenger ﷺ has explained that in the best of forms in the Hadith of Nu'maan bin Basheer: 'Certainly, the body has a morsel of flesh, when it is upright, all of the body is upright and when it is corrupted, all of the body is corrupted and that is the heart'..."See: the Introductory notes to *Riyadus-Saaliheen* by Maktabatus-Safa, 1424 AH, Cairo.

31 *Ilhaam* is: "that Allah puts into a person, something which prompts him to an action or abstinence; and it is a part of the revelation which Allah grants only some of whom He wills amongst His servants": *Al-Lisaan*: *Laam – Haa - Meem*

«And We inspired the mother of Musa (Moses), (saying): "Suckle him [Musa (Moses)], but when you fear for him, then cast him into the river and fear not, nor grieve. Verily! We shall bring him back to you, and shall make him one of (Our) Messengers»

Al-Qasas (Q28:7)

Likewise *at-Tahadduth*, being spoken to; that is, when the angels speak to a person. The Prophet ﷺ had said, "There were from those who came before you from the Children of Israel, those who were spoken to while they were not prophets. If they are in my *Ummah* (community) then Umar (is from them)".[32]

And like bravery, good dreams and things like that.

4. The Heart's Thoughts Could Salvage or Ruin a Person

A noble thought could come to a person's mind and he becomes saved. Likewise, a bad desire could enter somebody's mind and he becomes destroyed. An example is the report concerning the woman who was destroyed. The Prophet ﷺ said: "A woman from the Children of Israel entered the Fire because of her cat which she did not feed or allow to eat from the *Khashaash* of the earth".[33]

On the other hand, a noble thought crossed the mind of another woman and she gained salvation. The Prophet ﷺ said, "An adulteress saw a dog on a hot day wandering about

32 Reported by Imam Al-Bukhaari in his *Sahih*: the Book of The Virtues of the Companions: Chapter on The Virtues of Umar bin Al-Khattaab رضي الله عنه: 5/15

33 Reported by Imam Muslim in his *Sahih*, The Book of the Eclipse: The Chapter on What was Shown to the Prophet ﷺ of Paradise and the Hell: 6/510. The *Khashaash* are: the vermin and pests. See the last reference.

a well, letting out its tongue due to severe thirst. She fetched it water with her shoes and she was forgiven".[34]

5. The Heart's Uprightness Shows Uprightness of the Individual and the Society

The upright mind is the first brick in the uprightness of the society since the uprightness of the individual is preconditioned on the uprightness of his heart. The Prophet ﷺ said, "Certainly, the body has a morsel of flesh, when it is upright, all of the body is upright and when it is corrupted, all of the body is corrupted and that is the heart".[35]

Uprightness is of two forms: Physical and Spiritual. As for the physical uprightness, if the heart of a man is rectified, his body soon becomes refined. He will keep away from intoxicants, hard drugs and shameful deeds. So, when his body is rectified, he is a 'right brick' in the upliftment of the Muslim society and the establishment of its civilization. This is a major physical uprightness.

As regards the Spiritual rectification; the uprightness of the heart results in the proper fulfillment of the Rights of Allah the Mighty and Sublime like the prayer, fasting, partaking in the *Jihad* and spreading the *Da'wah*.

The nations will only put the hearts right by putting the actions right. However, the actions of the heart are acts of worship unique to the *Ummah* of Islam, if it had done well in these acts of worship, it would have established itself on the throne of the world's civilization.

From the foregoing, it becomes clear that the heart has

---

34 Reported by Imam Muslim in his *Sahih*: The Book of Greeting: the Chapter on The Virtue of Giving Water to the Beasts And feeding Them:14/402

35 Reported by Imam Al-Bukhaari and its reference had preceded.

peculiarities and great virtues. Therefore, it is obligatory to devote attention to its rectification and purification at all times; it should be watched closely so that it does not deviate or go astray.

Chapter 3
Foundations of the Heart's Worship

The heart's actions are divided into *Waajibaat* (Obligatory), *Mustahabbaat* (Supererogatory), and *Muharramah* (Prohibited), *Makroohaat* (Disliked) and *Mubaahaat* (Permissible). That is, the five rulings of Legal Responsibility also include the Heart's acts of worship.

The acts of worship which are obligatory upon the heart are, for example: *Al-Ikhlaas* (Sincerity), *at-Tawakkul* (Reliance on Allah), *Al-Khawf* (Fear of Allah), *ar-Rajaa* (Hope in Allah) and *At-Tawbah* (Repentance).[36]

Each of these acts of worship has two aspects: The basic deserving obligatory aspect (*Waajib*) and the perfecting and beloved (*Mustahabb*) aspect which is the degree of the *Muqarraboon* (the nearest, most beloved servants of Allah).

On the other hand, the *Mustahabb* heart-related acts of worship are like the (person's) perfection of the aforementioned obligatory heart-related worship, and like: *Ar-Ridaa* (Being pleased with Allah), *Al-Khushoo'* (Devoutness), longing for Allah the Mighty and Sublime, being close and dedicating oneself to Him.

---

36 Explanations shall soon come on these heart-related acts of worship – Allah willing.

As for the prohibited matters which affect the heart; they are divided into three:

1. *Kufr* (Disbelief); for example – *Ilhaad* (atheism), *Shirk* (polytheism) and *Shakk* (Doubting).

2. The *Kabaair* (Major sins): For example – *Ar-Riyaa* (Show-off), *Al-'Ujub* (Self-importance), *Al-Kibr* (Arrogance), *Al-Fakhar* (Pride), despair of Allah's favour, feeling safe from Allah's punishment, delight at the harm of Muslims and gloating over their grief and envy.

3. The *Sagaair* (Minor sins): They are the prohibited matters that are not up to being from the Major sins. For example, desiring and craving for some minor sins.

As for the disliked matters that affect the heart, they are its being busy away from Allah the Mighty and Sublime by its excessive connection with the worldly affairs. Likewise, the thoughts that cross the mind which one can prevent; avoiding such thoughts is better than thinking about them but thinking about them has no punishments.

As for the matters that are Permissible for the heart, they include its being empty of lofty ideas and its been filled with the engrossing worldly thoughts.

For the fact that the heart is of such great importance, as explained above, I would like to present the sections that follow to show – Allah willing – the importance of the Heart's acts of worship.

Chapter 4

Superiority of the Worship of the Heart over that of the Limbs'

The Limbs' acts of worship are of great importance; they are the pillars of Islam, the pointers to *Iman* and the ladder to *Ihsan*. They are the open signs of the uprightness of a person in his religion. However, these do not prevent the Heart's worship being of greater significance, more far-reaching effects, and more beautifully practiced.

This is owing to the fact that it is the heart helps in nearness to Allah (the Exalted). It is devoted to Him and its light from worship only spread through the limbs. Also, it is the heart that actually disobeys Allah; what gets to the limbs are from its own shamelessness and its consequences. It is the place of knowledge and piety, love and hatred, suspicions and doubts. It is the knower of Allah and that which strives towards Him. The limbs are only followers and servants of the heart.

The pious predecessors achieved great success and were really foremost – out of Allah's favour on them – due to their excelling in the Heart's worship and their uniqueness in this aspect is without equal as shall be explained – Allah willing.

From the comparisons that follow, the great excellence of the Heart's worship over those of the limbs is demonstrated:

4.1 First: Absence of the Heart's Acts of Worship Destroys the Limbs' Worship

This is an important and serious matter. The absence of *Ikhlaas* (sincerity) – for example – could lead to *Shirk* (polytheism) or *Nifaaq* (hypocrisy) bwhich destroy all the Limbs' worship. On the other hand, the absence of the Limbs' worship does not remove a person from his religion, based on the position of the majority of the scholars.

From the forms of the destruction of the Limbs' worship when the Heart's worship is absent are:

1. **Absence of Sincerity**

   It is the worst and most dangerous form. And that is because it could lead a person to *Shirk* and major hypocrisy – And the is with Allah. This important heart worship will be explained in details – Allah willing, in the next section.

2. **Pride**

   It is a pointer to the absence of humility which is a great heart-related worship. It basically prevents (its victim) from entrance to Paradise, no matter the servant's good and beautiful deeds – except as Allah wills – or if the proud repents. The Prophet ﷺ had said, "The one who has a grain weight of pride in his heart will not enter Paradise."[37]

3. Envy

It is a pointer to the absence of loving good for the Muslims which is a great heart-related worship. Envy destroys a person's good deeds owing to the burning fire he directs at his Muslim brother. The most chosen one ﷺ had warned, "Beware of envy; it envy eats up good deeds as fire burns up the firewood" – or he said - "the grass."[38]

4.2 Second: The Heart's Worship Leads to Salvation from Hell and Attainment of Paradise

Tawheed (the Oneness of Allah) is a heart-related worship. The Prophet ﷺsaid: "Whoever testifies that there is no deity worthy of worship except Allah Alone, without any partner, and that Muhammad is His servant and Messenger, and that 'Eesa is a servant of Allah and His Messenger and His word and His spirit (which He created) and that Paradise is true, and that the Fire is true; Allah will make him enterParadise on whatever action he performed."[39]

37 Reported by Imam Muslim in his *Sahih*: The Book of *Eeman*: The Chapter on The Prohibition of Pride: 2/268

38 Reported by Imam Abu Dawud in his *Sunan*: the Book of Etiquettes: the Chapter on Envy; and Ibn Maajah reported it in a similar form in the Book of Ascetics: the Chapter on Envy. The Hadith, putting together both chains of transmission, is *Hasan* (good) – Allah willing.

39 Reported by Imam Al-Bukhaari in his *Sahih*: The Book of the Prophets: The Chapter on His Saying: **"When the Angel said: 'O Maryam'"** - to His saying: **"Be; and he was"**.

Abu Sa'eed Al-Khudree ﷺ said: "The Messenger of Allah ﷺ said: 'The people of Paradise will see the people of the apartments above them as you see the far-away brilliant stars in the horizons from the east or the west due to the superiority of one over another.'. They asked, 'O Messenger of Allah! Are those the degrees of the Prophets, that none reaches except them?' He answered, 'Certainly, and by the One in whose hand is my soul, men[40] who believed in Allah and followed the Messengers.'"[41]

From the heart-related worship by which Paradise could be attained includes having good thoughts about the Muslims:

Only a few serve Allah (the Exalted) by this heart-related worship. Anas bin Maalik ﷺ said[42]: "We were sitting with Allah's Messenger ﷺ and he said, 'A man from the people of Paradise will come to you now.' One man from the *Ansaar*, from whose beard water trickled from his ablution…On the

40 i.e. **"…and a people…"** as is in the wording of Imam At-Tirmidhi in his *Sunan*: the Book of the Description of Paradise from Allah's Messenger ﷺ : the Chapter on The People of Paradise's seeing One Another in the Apartments. **(TN)**

41 Reported by Imam Muslim in his *Sahih*: the Book of Paradise and the Description of Its Delight and People: The Book of Showing the *Ridwaan* on the people of Paradise: 17/301.

42 "…it has a broken chain between Az-Zuhree (who was said to have reported from Anas) and Anas; between them both is a reporter not mentioned as said by Haafidh Hamza Al-Kannaanee as quoted by Haafidh Al-Mizzee in *Tuhfat ul-Ashraaf* (1/395) and then, An-Naajee who then said (2/198): 'And this defect was not taken note of by the author' I say: Abdur-Razzaaq reported it in *Al-Musannaf* (11/287/20559) and through his route, many others, from them, Ahmad, and he (Abdur-Razaaq) said: Ma'mar narrated to us from Az-Zuhree who said: 'Anas bin Maalik narrated to me'. This chain is apparently reliable and Al-'Iraaqee ruled based on it in *Takhreej ul-Ihyaa* (3/187) and we also did that over sometime before the defect became known…As such, Al-Haafidh (Ibn Hajar Al-'Asqalaanee) said after stating it in *An-Nukkah Az-Zaraaf 'alaa Al-Atraaf*: it has been known that it has defect.'" See *At-Targeeb wat-Tarheeb* by Abdul-'Azeem Al-Mundhiree (3/1065) (Published by Maktabat ul-Ma'aarif, Riyadh. 1424 AH) **(TN)**

following day, the Prophet ﷺ said something similar to that, and that same man came, like the first time.

On the third day, the Prophet ﷺ made a similar statement again and that same man came as he did the first time. When the Prophet ﷺ stood up, Abdullah bin 'Umar followed him and said, 'I got in a dispute with my father. So, I swore not to go to him for three days. Perhaps, you may wish to accommodate me for the while? The man said: 'Yes.'"

Anas said: "Abdullah used to narrate that he stayed with him for those three nights and could not find him performing the late-night prayers except that when he woke up in the night, he remembers Allah the Mighty and Sublime and says the *Takbeer* (the saying, *Allahu Akbar*, meaning – Allah is the Greatest) until he prays the *Fajr* Prayer". Abdullah said: "Except that I never heard him speak except good.

When the third day reached and I was about not giving much consideration to his deeds, I said (to him): 'O servant of Allah, there had not been anything of annoyance or forsaking between myself and my father, but I heard Allah's Messenger ﷺ saying to us, three times, *A man from the people of Paradise will come on to you*, and you came in three times. So, I wanted to stay with you to watch your deeds perhaps take after you. But I did not find you doing great deeds. So, how did you achieve what Allah's Messenger ﷺ said about you?' The man replied, 'It was just what you saw.'

When I turned to go, he called me and said, 'It was just what you saw, except that I do not cheat anyone or envy anyone for a favour Allah has granted him.' So, Abdullah said, 'This was how you achieved what was said about you and it is what we are unable to achieve.'"[43]

4.3 Third: High rank is Attained in Paradise from the Heart's Worship

There are many texts explaining the greatness of the reward for the Heart's worship and the high rank of its people - those who worship by it - in Paradise while its like has not been mentioned for the Limbs' worship despite their importance and excellence. From those acts of worship (related to the heart of which great rewards are mentioned) is loving Allah the Mighty and Sublime and yearning for Him, relying on Him, turning to Him and seeking help from Him. Each of these has great rewards leading to the attainment of high degrees in His Paradise.

From that also is, loving for the sake of Allah (the Exalted) which is also clearly a heart-related worship:

Ibn Abbas ﷺ (may Allah be pleased with them both) said,[44] "Allah's Messenger ﷺ said, 'Allah has some people who will sit on the Day of Judgment on the right side of the *'Arsh* – and the both of His Hands are right – on platforms of light. Their faces will be from light and they are not Prophets or martyrs or the *Siddeeqoon* (truthful ones).' It was asked, 'O Messenger of Allah! Who are they?' He answered, 'They are

43 Imam Al-Haythamee said: 'Reported by Ahmad and Al-Bazzaar...and its reporters are those of authentic narrations': See: *Majmu' uz-Zawaaid*: 8/81-82.

44 *Sahih* (authentic): See *At-Targeeb wat-Tarheeb* by Abdul-'Azeem Al-Mundhiree (3/1106) (Published by Maktabat ul-Ma'aarif, Riyadh. 1424 AH) **(TN)**

those who loved one another for the greatness of Allah the Mighty and Sublime."[45]

From that also is good character because it entails many of the heart-related acts of worship such as humility, freeing the mind of grudge, thinking positively of people, mercy, taking things easy with the people and many things like that.

Abu Dardaa رضي الله عنه said that, "The Prophet ﷺ said, 'There is nothing weightier in the *Meezaan*[46] of a believer on the Day of Judgment as good character.'"[47] He ﷺ also said: "Certainly, from the most beloved to me among you, who will seat nearest to me of the Day of Resurrection, are the best of you in character."[48]

The prophets have greatly excelled because they outclassed all in the heart-related worship: Ibraaheem (*alayh as-Salaat was-Salaam*) greatly relied on Allah, Ayoob (*alayh as-Salaat was-Salaam*) was very patient, Aadam (*alayh as-Salaat was-Salaam*) sought sincere repentance, 'Eesaa (*alayh as-Salaat was-Salaam*) practised much of abandoning the worldly pleasures to seek closeness to Allah which is purely from the heart-related worship, and our Prophet, Muhammad ﷺ, had been favoured with all these and others from the heart-related worship in the best and most perfect forms. Thus,

45 Imam Haythamee said: "Reported by At-Tabraanee, and its reporters are mentioned to be trustworthy": See *Majmu' uz-Zawaaid*: 10/280. The Hadith is widely known, reported in many books through many routes with similar wordings.

46 That is, the weight upon which deeds shall be considered on the Day of Resurrection.

47 Reported by Imam At-Tirmidhi in his *Sunan*: The Book of Ascetics; the Chapter on what is reported about Good Character, and said: a *Hasan-Sahih* Hadith.

48 Reported by Imam At-Tirmidhi in his *Sunan*: The Book of Ascetics: The Chapter on What is Reported Regarding Sublime Characters, and said: A *Hasan-Gareeb* Hadith. The Hadith is *Hasan* (good) – Allah willing. See: *Tuhfat ul-Ahwadhee* (6/160).

they were entitled to the high levels and ranks – may Allah's peace and abundant blessings be upon them.

4.4 Fourth: The Heart's Worship is More Difficult than the Limbs'

It is therefore, greater and more virtuous than the Limbs' acts of worship. Likewise, the sins of the heart, like *Shirk* (associating partners with Allah) and *Nifaaq* (hypocrisy) are far worse than the sins the limbs commit. To demonstrate the difficulty of some of The Heart's worship, I will state a statement of one of the *Taabi'oon*: Yoonus bin 'Ubayd.[49]

One of his students wrote to him to ask questions. So, Yunus replied, "Your letter got to me. You were asking that I should write to you about my condition. So, I say that, I offered my soul to love for the people, what it loves for itself, and detest for them, what it detests for itself but it did not achieve it. Then, I offered it another time, to leave mentioning them except with good but I found fasting on a very hot day easier upon it than that. This is my situation – O my brother – *was-Salaam*."[50]

4.5 Fifth: The Heart's Worship is More Beautiful than the Limbs' Worship

The worship of the limbs are of the greatest importance – as said earlier – but that does not negate the heart-related worship being more encompassing and more pleasing in their impact, effect and practice. This is what a person feels

49 From Basra, a great scholar, model and dependable from the younger *Taabi'een* and among their nobles. See *Nuzhat ul-Fudalaa*: 1/539.

50 The last reference.

in himself if his soul is righteous and attached to its Lord the Mighty and Sublime.

One of the *Salaf* said, "The poor from the people of the world (are those who) left it and did not taste the best of what it contains." They asked, "What is the best thing it contains?" He remarked, "Love of Allah, the desire to meet Him, being devoted to Him and turning away from other than Him."[51]

The heart-related acts of worship beautify those of the limbs. Hence, the difference is great between prayer performed with a conscious mind and that performed by a heedless and forgetful mind; and between fasting with sincerity, devotion and the yearning for reward and fasting devoid of all that. Likewise, there is wide difference between pilgrimage performed with humility and reverence and pilgrimage with arrogance and pride, and so on.

4.6 Sixth: The Heart's Deeds are More Rewarding and Effective than the Limbs' Deeds

The *Salaf* رضي الله عنهم preferred the Heart's worship over engaging in much worshiping with the limbs. Below are some of their statements about contemplating about the signs of Allah (the Exalted) and the hereafter which is a noble heart-related worship:

Abu Dardaa[52] رضي الله عنه said, "Contemplating for an hour is better

51 *Tahdheeb Madaarij is-Saalikeen*: pg 245

52 He is the eminent companion, 'Uwaymir bin Zayd bin Qays Al-Ansari. He died in Damascus in the year 23 AH. See *Nuzhat ul-Fudalaa*: 1/157-161

than the late-night prayer."[53] Umm Dardaa[54] was asked, "In which worship was Abu Dardaa most frequent?" She replied, "Contemplation and deep thought."[55]

The worship of a group of people was described to Sa'eed bin Al-Musayyib[56] ﵀ that they engage in prayers after the *Zuhr* (forenoon) prayer until the *'Asr* (afternoon) prayer. He remarked, "But by Allah, that is not worship in anyway. Worship is contemplating about the signs of Allah and abstaining from His prohibitions."[57]

Yusuf bin Asbaat said, "Sufyaan said to me after the *'Ishaa* (the night) prayer, 'Bring me the container so that I make the ablution.' So, I gave it to him. He took it with his right hand and placed his left hand on his cheek and started contemplating. I slept and then woke up at the time of the *Fajr* (early-morning) prayer and the container was still in his hand as it was. Then I asked, 'It is dawn!' He said, 'I have been contemplating about the hereafter since you gave me the container until this hour.'"[58]

Similarly, the heart-related worship leads to the attainment of *Ihsan* which is the greatest rank in the *Deen* which is the desire of the learned and the struggle of the pious. That is because *Ihsan* is built upon self-appraisal which is purely a heart-related worship. The Prophet ﷺ defined *Ihsan*. He

53 The last reference.

54 Hujaymah Al-Awsaabiyyah Al-Humayriyyah Ad-Dimashqiyyah, the younger Umm Dardaa. See the last reference: 1/370-377.

55 The previous reference: 1/160.

56 The scholar of the people of Madeenah, and the leader of the *Taabi'een* in his time; he died in the year 94 AH. See the previous reference: 1/376.

57 The previous reference: 1/376. This is only understood to imply preference for the heart-related worship and not that these acts are not from worship itself. **(TN)**

58 The previous reference: 1/584.

said, "That you worship Allah, as though you see Him, for if you do not see Him, certainly, He sees you."[59]

4.7 Seventh: The Heart's Worship Agitates and Stimulates the Limbs

This is because as *Iman*, the Oneness of Allah and the love of Allah increase in the heart, it stirs the limbs to worship. Utbah - the young-man[60] said, "Anyone who knows Allah will love Him, and the one who loves Him will worship Him."[61]

And this is something manifest and known, there is no need stating evidences to establish it. One knows deep in his heart that when his heart is upright, he makes more efforts in the prayers and fasting and when his heart is corrupted or weak, his acts of worship are also few and his limbs become tired.

4.8 Eighth: The Heart's Worship Magnifies the Limbs' Worship

From the examples of that is the intention. It has great impact on the perfection and multiplication of the Limbs' worship. Even, the Limbs' worship are not right without it! Imam Abdullah bin Al-Mubarak[62] said, "Many a simple

59 A part of a Hadith reported by Imam Al-Bukhaaree in his *Sahih*: The Book of *Iman*: The Chapter on Jibril's Question on *Iman* and *Ihsan* and the Knowledge of the Hour.

60 Utbah bin Aban Al-Basree, the ascetic and pious. He attained martyrdom – Allah willing – in the Battle of Rome. See *Nuzhat ul-Fudalaa*: 1/564.

61 The previous reference.

62 The ascetic, ardent servant, the leader, the great scholar of Hadith Abdullah bin Al-Mubarak bin Waadih Al-Marwazee. He died in the year 181 AH. See the previous reference: 2/260-264.

good deed is magnified by the intention. And many a big deed is made insignificant by the intention."[63] And the intention is purely a heart-related worship, not of the limbs.

4.9 Ninth: The Heart's Worship May Substitute the Limbs' Worship

The heart-related acts of worship could take the place of the Limbs' in some situations specifically mentioned by the Law-Giver (the Exalted) and from that is the *Jihad*. The Prophet ﷺ said, "Whoever dies without having engaged in a battle and neither intends it, dies upon a form of hypocrisy."[64]

Thus, intending to engage in *Jihad* and determining and having it in mind takes the place of the engagement – Allah willing – if (in the end) the person could not engage in *Jihad* for one reason or the other. The Prophet ﷺ had said, "Whoever truly asks Allah for martyrdom, Allah brings him to the level of the martyrs even when he dies on his bed."[65] And the place of truthfulness about asking for martyrdom is the heart and no other.

Likewise the prohibition of evil; the Prophet ﷺ said, "Whoever amongst you who sees an evil should change it with his hand, and if he is not able, then, with his tongue; and if he is not able then by his heart…"[66]

---

63 The previous reference: 1/657.

64 Reported by Imam Muslim in his *Sahih*: The Book on Leadership: The Chapter on whoever dies Never Intending to Engage in Battle:13/50.

65 Reported by Imam Muslim in his *Sahih*: the Book on Leadership: The Chapter on The Recommendation to Seek Martyrdom on the Cause of Allah, the Most High: 13/49.

66 Reported by Imam Muslim in his *Sahih*: The Book on *Iman*: the Chapter on the Obligation of commanding Good and Prohibiting Evil: 2/217.

4.10 Tenth: The Limbs' Actions Have Known Limits but the Hearts' are Limitless

That is because, the actions of the limbs – no matter how much or great -, have known time and specific limits. But when the acts of worship envelope the heart of a person, and he adopts them, they become things he adheres to during his wakefulness and sleep, good health and illness, calmness and worry and in all his affairs.

An example of that is the love for Allah the Mighty and Sublime and being pleased with Him, extolling Him and being sincere to Him. If the servant becomes engrossed in these and adheres to them, how much good would he reap, and in how many manifolds will his rewards be?! This is not for the acts of the limbs which stop, in many instances, right in the lifetime of the servant, no matter his efforts. The period of sleep, engagement in the regular worldly activities, attending to personal and family needs are enough periods of its stoppage.

4.11 Eleventh: Some of the Heart's Worship Continues Even When the Limbs' Worship Stops or Reduces

The Muslim is asked regarding the *Tawheed* in his grave: and *Tawheed* is purely an heart-related act of worship. The two angels will ask him about his Lord, his Prophet, and his religion. The believer will give the best response while the hypocrite and the unbeliever will be unable to.

Even in Paradise, the Heart's worship do not stop. In Paradise, the Muslim will still love Allah (the Exalted), know Him in the best manner, and extol Him. These and its like are from the greatest heart-related acts of worship.

On the other hand, there is not in Paradise from the Limbs' worship except the *Tasbeeh* (Allah's glorification) with the tongue which will be due to the perfection of the greatness of Allah in the hearts of the people of Paradise which is a heart's worship. The Prophet ﷺ said, "The people of Paradise will eat and drink in it. They will not spit or urinate or excrete feaces or blow their noses. Rather, their food will be groats like the oozing of the musk. They will recite the *Tasbeeh* and the *Hamd* repeatedly as the breath is made repeatedly."[67]

'Ibaadah (Worship) should not be mixed up with legal responsibility since *'Ibaadah* is much more encompassing than it. So, it is - as its meaning had preceded, an all-encompassing word for all what Allah likes and is pleased with of statements and actions whether open and secret, and is obtainable in Paradise as explained. As for legal responsibility, it stops at death – And Allah knows Best.

From the foregoing, it becomes clear that the heart-related acts of worship are superior to those of the limbs. They are more excellent in their beauty, impact and impression on the soul. Therefore one should check his soul and value its state. The above discussions should also make one hasten towards rectifying his soul whenever it is tired or weak or when it errs because it is the controller of the limbs, their leader and their propeller (whose weakness portends great danger for the individual). Allah knows Best.

---

67 Reported by Imam Muslim in his Sahih: The Book Of Paradise And The Descriptions Of Its Pleasure And Its People: 17/304.

Chapter 5
How to Enliven the Hearts

The living heart that regularly remembers Allah is from the favours of Allah (the Exalted) on the servant. So the person with a dead heart could be (considered) dead before his actual death since there is no goodness or benefit in his existence!

The things that help enliven the heart include:

1. **Remembrance of Allah, (the Exalted)**

   Its benefits are known and the one who regularly and consciously remembers Allah, his heart does not become corrupt or dead. The Prophet ﷺ said: "The like of the one that remembers his Lord and the one who does not make remembrance is that of the living and the dead."[68]

2. **Regularly Remembering Death**

   This is because the one who regularly remembers death has fewer expectations, lots of deeds and few sins. Sa'eed bin Jubayr[69] رحمه الله said, "If the remembrance of death were

68 Reported by Imam Al-Bukhaari: The Book of Supplications: The Chapter on The Excellence of The Remembrance of Allah – The Mighty and Sublime.

69 He is the Imam, the great scholar of *Tafseer* from Kufah. Al-Hajjaaj killed him in the year 95 AH. See *Nuzhat ul-Fudalaa*: 1/393-396.

to leave my heart I would be afraid that my heart is corrupted."[70]

3. **Visiting the Graveyard**

This a good almost completely abandoned. Most of those to be ascribed with piety might have forgotten it let, alone the common people. It is from the greatest means of enlivening the heart and connecting it with the All-Knower of Secrets towards which the pious predecessors hastened.[71]

Safwaan bin Sulaym[72] came to Baqee' and one of the pious people saw him and followed him saying (to himself), "I will see what he will do." He said: "So, Safwaan sat near a grave and continued to cry until I felt pity for him and thought that it was the grave of a member of his household. He passed by me at another time and I followed him and he sat near the grave of a different person. So, I mentioned that to Muhammad bin Munkadir.[73] I said: I had thought that it was the grave of a member of his family to which Muhammad said, "They are all his family and brothers. He is a man

---

70 The previous reference: 1/394.

71 Visiting the graveyards based on its etiquettes is known and established in the religion and what is mentioned here should not in anyway be misconstrued to mean grave worship – seeking help from the dead in the graves, which is forbidden and is known to be from the aspects of association of partners with Allah - *Shirk*. **(TN)**

72 The trustworthy Imam, a great scholar of Hadith and an erudite scholar of Jurisprudence. He died in the year 132 AH at age 72. See the previous reference: 1/498-499

73 The Imam, great scholar of Hadith, and trustworthy. He was born in thirty-some years AH and he died in the year 130 AH. See the previous reference: 1/495-497.

who enlivens his heart through the remembrance of the dead each time it becomes hard.'"[74]

4. **Visiting the Pious and Knowing their Good Deeds**

   This is a very beneficial thing to do. However, if it is not easily attainable then one should visit them and find out about them from the books that expound their life histories. Ja'afar bin Sulayman said, "When I notice my heart being hard, I go and look at the face of Muhammad bin Waasi'.[75] It used to be as if he was bereaved of a child."

One should regularly watch over his heart so that it is not overtaken by delusion and the shameful deeds related to the heart like show-off and *Shirk*. Abu Hafs An-Nisaburi[76] said, "I watched over my heart for twenty years and then, it kept watch over me for twenty years."

Then, one should keep away from the things that corrupt the heart some of which will be discussed in the next section – Allah willing.

---

74 The previous reference: 1/498.

75 The devout Imam, a model - Abu Bakr Al-Azdee Al-Basree, one of the most eminent among the *Tabi'een*. He died in the year 123 AH. See *Nuzhat ul-Fudalaa*: 1/526-527.

76 The Imam, a model, the scholar of Khurasaan – 'Amr bin Salam An-Nisaburi, the ascetic. He died in the year 264 AH. See the previous reference: 2/913-914.

Chapter 6

Things that Corrupt the Hearts

The heart gets corrupted as the body gets corrupted, and its corruption is from many things that come upon the servant such as:

1. **Occupying the Heart with and Connecting it to Other than Allah**

   The things that distract the heart are many such as love of the world, very high hopes, seeking the failures of people, disliking them, seeking to make reprisals on them and filling the heart with grudge against them. When will the one with such a heart connect his heart to Allah (the Exalted)? And when will he leave these obsessions?

   This is in addition to what the person falls into – due to all these – of fewer remembrance of Allah the Mighty and Sublime.

2. **Sins**

   Its impact in the darkening of the heart thickening of his veil away from Allah the Mighty and Sublime is well-known. Allah (the Exalted) said:

كَلَّاۖ بَلۡۜ رَانَ عَلَىٰ قُلُوبِهِم مَّا كَانُواْ يَكۡسِبُونَ ١٤

«Nay! But on their hearts is the *Raan* (covering of sins and evil deeds) which they used to earn.»

Al-Mutaffifin (Q83:14)

Raan is explained by what is reported from Abu Hurayrah ﵁ who said, "The Prophet ﷺ said, "When the believer commits a sin, it becomes a black spot in his heart. If he repents and abandons the sin and seeks forgiveness, his heart is polished. But if he persists, it gets bigger until it (the spot) covers his heart. That is the *Raan* that Allah – the Mighty and Sublime -mentioned in:

كَلَّاۖ بَلۡۜ رَانَ عَلَىٰ قُلُوبِهِم مَّا كَانُواْ يَكۡسِبُونَ ١٤

«Nay! But on their hearts is the *Raan* (covering of sins and evil deeds) which they used to earn.»[77]

Al-Mutaffifin (Q83:14)

Imam Al-Hasan Al-Basree said, "It is sin upon sin until it blinds the soul and it dies!"[78]

3. Much Mingling with People

This is because the yardstick of praiseworthy mingling

77 Imam Ahmad reported the Hadith in his *Musnad*; and the teacher, Al-Bannah said: "It is reported by An-Nasaaee, At-Tirmidhi, Ibn Maajah, and Ibn Jareer, and At-Tirmidhi said: 'This is a *HasanSahih* Hadith'". See the previous reference.

78 *Tafseer ul-Qur'aan il-'Azeem*: 8/373.

is cooperating with the people upon goodness, not to cooperate with them in sins and excessively indulging in permissible matters. Whoever has to relate with the people in permissible matters, he should pull out his heart as the hair is removed from the dough.

He should be with them; present, but absent, near but far, asleep but in wakefulness, looking at them but not seeing them, hearing their words but not preserving it by heart. This is because his heart could be taken while he is amongst them and taken up to the esteemed companions together with the pure souls.[79]

4. **Excessive eating and drinking**

Fudayl bin 'Iyyaad[80] said, "Two traits harden the heart: Excessive speech and excessive food."[81] Imam Ash-Shafi'i said, "I have not eaten to fill for sixteen years except once. So, I inserted my hand (into my mouth) and disgorged it because satiety makes the body weighty, hardens the heart, takes away the intelligence, brings about excessive sleep and makes one weak for worship."[82]

Abu Sulayman Ad-Daaraanee[83] said: "Everything rusts and the rust of the heart is eating to fill."[84]

---

79 See: *Tahdheeb Madaarij is-Saalikeen*: pg 246.

80 He is the Imam, the model, the trustworthy, Shaykh ul-Islaam, Abu Ali At-Tameemee, the neighbor of Allah's sanctified place. See Nuzhat ul-Fudalaa: 2/660-670.

81 *Nuzhatul-Fudalaa*: 2/667.

82 *Nuzhat ul-Fudalaa*: 2/736.

83 The ascetic of his time, Abdur-Rahmaan bin Ahmad Al-'Ansee Ad-Daaraanee. He was born around 140 AH and he died in the year 215 AH. See the previous reference: 2/752-753.

84 The previous reference: 2/753.

5. **Excessive sleep**

People waste lots of time and that is due to their excessive sleep since the average person today sleeps for a third of his life-span. There are some of the people who exceed this; so, for how long will he sleep? If one is excessive and sleeps, leaving off obligations, his heart dies – And the refuge is with Allah.

PART 2

Some Basic Heart-Related Worship

After discussing the heart and defining it, and explaining its excellence and the importance of its acts of worship, I consider it appropriate to explain the major heart-related acts of worship so that you could know its significance and excellence.

Therefore, I have mentioned five heart-related acts of worship around which – and Allah knows best – actions revolve. They are:

1. *Al-Ikhlaas* (Sincerity)

2. *At-Tawbah* (Repentance)

3. *At-Tawakkul* (Reliance on Allah)

4. *Al-Khawf* (Fear of Allah) and

5. *Ar-Rajaa* (Hope in Allah).

Thereafter, I followed it with the mentioning of some important basic characters connected to the heart and its acts of worship as examples of other beautiful characters and enviable attributes.

Extensive discussions had preceded on the heart-related acts of worship because it is the basis for the actions of the limbs. So if they are upright, the actions are upright and the characters are improved upon. We ask Allah (the Exalted) to make the Muslims, including us, achieve these worship and characters in speech and action, condition and consequence so that we succeed in this world and the hereafter treading the path of the accepted and sincere ones.

Chapter 7
Al-Ikhlas (Sincerity)

It is the greatest heart-related act of worship and the most dangerous. Many verses, Hadith and narrations from the pious predecessors have explained its excellence and warned regarding its neglect.

7.1 Lexical meaning

A thing is (said to be) *Kha-la-sa*, *Ya-kh-lu-su* – *Khu-loo-san* and *Khu-laa-san* when it had gotten stuck but was then saved, and it became safe (from danger). The *Mukhlis*: is one who sincerely declares Allah's oneness; and *Al-Mukhlis* (is also): one, saved by Allah: Allah picked him out, safe from filth. Thus, the Statement of *Ikhlaas* (Sincerity): is the Statement of *At-Tawheed*.

Al-Ikhlaas (Sincerity) in action is: abandoning show-off.[85]

Technically:

The devout scholars have a number of beautiful statements regarding sincerity such as:

85 See: *Lisaan ul-'Arab*: *Khaa- Laam – Saad*.

1. The evenness of the actions of the servant in the open and in secret.

2. Sincerity is not to seek a witness for your deeds except Allah and not one who recompenses besides Him.

3. Making actions free from the observations of the creatures.[86]

- Sincerity has levels and ranks, one above the other. From it is that one's hidden is greater than his open since sincerity already becomes established by the evenness of the hidden and the open. However, its highest level is when the hidden is greater.

- Sincerity is from the hidden actions, invisible to people. So, no angel knows it so that he could write it or any devil so that he destroys it.[87] The Prophet ﷺ had said,[88] "A sealed scroll shall be brought on the Day of Resurrection and it will be spread open before Allah (the Exalted). He the Mighty and Sublime will say: 'Throw this away and take this.' The angels will say, 'By Your Might and Sublimity, we only saw (in him) goodness.' Then, Allah the Mighty and Sublime will say, 'Certainly, this was for other than me and I will only accept what (was done) to seek my face.'"[89]

---

86 *Tahdheeb Madaarij is-Saalikeen*: pg 322.

87 See the previous reference.

88 This narration is graded *Da'eef* (weak) by Al-Albaanee. He said: "The report of Al-Bayhaqee (which was also mentioned by Al-Mundhiree) and others have exposed the fact that the chain of transmission is mistaken and that it revolves around an unknown reporter (i.e. who is not known to be a trustworthy reporter) and … " *See At-Targeeb wat-Tarheeb* (1/78) by Al-Maktabat ul-Ma'aarif, Riyadh. **(TN)**

89 Haafidh Al-Mundhiree said: "It is reported by Al-Bazzaar and At-Tabaree with two chains; the narrators of one of them are all reliable narrators". See *At-Targeeb wat-Tarheeb*: 1/73.

The verses on sincerity are many including:

وَمَآ أُمِرُوٓاْ إِلَّا لِيَعۡبُدُواْ ٱللَّهَ مُخۡلِصِينَ لَهُ ٱلدِّينَ ... ﴿٥﴾

«And they were commanded not, but that they should worship Allah, and worship none but Him Alone.»

Al-Bayyinah (Q98:5)

.... فَٱعۡبُدِ ٱللَّهَ مُخۡلِصٗا لَّهُ ٱلدِّينَ ﴿٢﴾ أَلَا لِلَّهِ ٱلدِّينُ .... ﴿٣﴾

«So worship Allah (Alone) by doing religious deeds sincerely for Allah's sake only. Surely, the religion (i.e. the worship and the obedience) is for Allah only.»

Az-Zumar (Q39:2-3)

.... فَمَن كَانَ يَرۡجُواْ لِقَآءَ رَبِّهِۦ فَلۡيَعۡمَلۡ عَمَلٗا صَٰلِحٗا وَلَا يُشۡرِكۡ بِعِبَادَةِ رَبِّهِۦٓ
أَحَدَۢا ﴿١١٠﴾

«So whoever hopes for the Meeting with his Lord, let him work righteousness and associate none as a partner in the worship of his Lord.»

Al-Kahf (Q18:110)

وَسَيُجَنَّبُهَا ٱلۡأَتۡقَى ﴿١٧﴾ ٱلَّذِي يُؤۡتِي مَالَهُۥ يَتَزَكَّىٰ ﴿١٨﴾ وَمَا لِأَحَدٍ عِندَهُۥ مِن
نِّعۡمَةٖ تُجۡزَىٰٓ ﴿١٩﴾ إِلَّا ٱبۡتِغَآءَ وَجۡهِ رَبِّهِ ٱلۡأَعۡلَىٰ ﴿٢٠﴾ وَلَسَوۡفَ يَرۡضَىٰ ﴿٢١﴾

«And *Al-Muttaqun* (the pious and righteous) will

be far removed from it (Hell). He who spends his wealth for increase in self-purification and has in his mind no favour from anyone for which a reward is expected in return, Except only the desire to seek the Countenance of his Lord, the Most High; he surely will be pleased (when he will enter Paradise).»

Al-Layl (Q92:17-21)

In a *Hadith-Qudsee*, Allah the Mighty and Sublime said, "I am the most Sufficient of partners away from *Shirk*. Whoever does any deed ascribing other than me with me regarding it, I will abandon him and his ascription." [90]

Ubayy bin Ka'b ﵁ said: "The Messenger of Allah (y) said, "Give glad tidings of commendation, prestige, religion, and establishment on the earth…to this *Ummah*." He said: "Whoever amongst them that brings up an act of the hereafter to seek the worldly benefits will not get any reward in the hereafter."[91]

Khaythamah bin Abdir-Rahmaan ﵁ said, "I was sitting with Abdullah bin 'Amr bin Al-'Aas and Abdullah bin 'Umar ﵁ and Abdullah bin 'Umar said, 'The *Shaytaan* moves in the body of the son of Aadam as the blood and soul move.' Abdullah bin 'Amr wept and then said, 'I heard the Messenger of Allah (y) saying: 'Whoever makes the people hear his deeds Allah will make him be heard by his creatures with it (i.e. the action) and its smallness and insignificance.''' [92]

---

90 Reported by Imam Muslim in his *Sahih*: The Book of Ascetism: The Chapter on the Prohibition of Show-off: Hadith number 2985.

91 Reported by Imam Ahmad and its narrators are reliable as mentioned by Imam Al-Haythamee in *Majma'u Az-Zawaaid*: 1/223.

92 Reported by Imam Ahmad and Tabaraanee and one of the chains of At-Tabaraanee in Al-Kabeer contain reliable reporters as is mentioned by Al-Haythamee in *Majma'u*: 1/225.

The pious predecessors ﵃ have greatly encouraged sincerity. Rabee' bin Khuthaym[93] said, "The secrets that are unknown to the people but are plain to Allah; seek their cure which your repenting from them without returning to them."[94] He ﵀ also said, "All of what the Face of Allah is not sought with fades away."[95]

7.2 Attaining Sincerity is Difficult

Sincerity is valuable, difficult to achieve and is unknown to many who are engaged in acts of worship. For this reason, the pious predecessors used to beseech Allah (the Exalted) for sincerity. Here is the leader, Ali bin Al-Husayn[96] ﵁ beseeching Allah (the Exalted), saying, "O Allah! I seek refuge in you from Your beautifying my open (deeds) to the viewing eyes and making ugly my hidden to the obscure eyes."[97]

He was only beseeching Allah for sincerity in actions because it is difficult to attain, and it is not granted except to the fortunate. "And sincerity is not perfected except with honesty and honesty cannot be achieved except with sincerity, and the both connot be gotten except with patience."[98] "It was said to one of the pious, 'What is the most difficult thing on the soul?' He answered, 'Sincerity; for it (the soul) has no share from it.'"[99]

93 One of the eminent *Taabi'een*; he lived at the period of the Prophet ﷺ but never met him. He died in the year 65 AH. See *Nuzhat ul-Fudalaa*: 1/370.

94 The previous reference.

95 The previous reference: 1/381.

96 The son of Ali ﵁; from the eminent servants and ascetics. He died in the year 94 AH in Madeenah. See *Nuzhat ul-Fudalaa*: 1/404.

97 The previous reference: 1/407.

98 *Tahdheeb Madaarij is-Saalikeen*: pg 322.

99 The previous reference.

Ayyub As-Sukhtiyaanee[100] said, "Making the intentions sincere for actions was most difficult upon them of all good deeds".[101] The Imam, the ascetic, Fudayl bin 'Iyyaad, explaining the difficulty in achieving sincerity and mentioning a matter which many of the servants engage in, said: "If it were said to you; 'O show-off', you get annoyed and it becomes unbearable to you. Perhaps, what was said to you is the truth. You have shown goodness for worldly benefits and pretended. You shortened your garment, bettered your *Sumt*[102] and kept away your harm until it was said: 'Abu So-and-so is a righteous servant, how good is his *Sumt*!' So, they will honour you, come to you and refer to you, like the *Satuk Dirham*;[103] not known by everyone but when it is opened up, copper is seen."[104]

7.3 Benefits and Impacts of Sincerity

Sincerity has some great importance, some of which are mentioned below:

1. It is the Pillar of Action and its Hump:

This is owing to the fact that the one who acts without sincerity is toiling, tiring out himself without reward; Allah – the most High – said:

---

100 From Basra, trustworthy and from the eminent among the pious predecessors. A number of people reported narrations from him. He died in the year 131 AH at age sixty-five. See *Ithaaf us-Saadat il-Muttaqeen*: 13/87-88.

101 The previous reference.

102 The appearance of the righteous people and their good sight: See *Lisaan ul-'Arab. Sin-Meem-Taa*

103 That is, the counterfeit *Dirham* that looks like silver but is actually of copper.

104 See: *Nuzhat ul-Fudalaa*: 2/667.

وَقَدِمْنَآ إِلَىٰ مَا عَمِلُواْ مِنْ عَمَلٍ فَجَعَلْنَٰهُ هَبَآءً مَّنثُورًا ﴿٢٣﴾

«And We shall turn to whatever deeds they (disbelievers, polytheists, sinners, etc.) did, and We shall make such deeds as scattered floating particles of dust.»

Al-Furqan (Q25:23)

The Prophet ﷺ said, "Certainly, the deeds are rewarded according to intentions and everyone shall be rewarded for what he intended. So, anyone whose migration is to (gain) the worldly benefit will attain it or for a woman, he will marry her; then, his migration is to what for which he migrated."[105]

The ascetic, Fudayl bin 'Iyyaad said regarding Allah's saying:

ٱلَّذِي خَلَقَ ٱلْمَوْتَ وَٱلْحَيَوٰةَ لِيَبْلُوَكُمْ أَيُّكُمْ أَحْسَنُ عَمَلًاۚ وَهُوَ ٱلْعَزِيزُ ٱلْغَفُورُ ﴿٢﴾

«Who has created death and life, that He may test you which of you is best in deed.»

Al-Mulk (Q67:2)

"It is the most sincere of it and the best of it." It was said: "O Abu Ali: 'What does that mean?' He said: "If an action is sincere but not right, it will not be accepted; and if it is right but not sincere, it will not be accepted until it is sincere and right. The sincere one is that for the sake of Allah and the

105 Reported by Al-Bukhaari in his *Sahih*.

right one is that which conforms with the *Sunnah*." Then, he recited:

.... فَمَن كَانَ يَرْجُوا۟ لِقَآءَ رَبِّهِۦ فَلْيَعْمَلْ عَمَلًا صَٰلِحًا وَلَا يُشْرِكْ بِعِبَادَةِ رَبِّهِۦٓ أَحَدًۢا ﴿١١٠﴾

«So whoever hopes for the Meeting] with his Lord, let him work righteousness and associate none as a partner in the worship of his Lord.»

Al-Kahf (Q18:110)

The Prophet ﷺ had informed us about the end of the one whose actions are not sincerely for Allah (the Exalted). He spoke regarding it in a great Hadith reported from him by Abu Hurayrah رضي الله عنه and narrated from Abu Hurayrah by Shufayy Al-Asbahee who said, "I entered Madeenah and saw a man around whom the people gathered. I enquired, 'Who is this?' They replied, 'Abu Hurayrah'.

So, I went closer to him until I sat before him while he was narrating to the people. When he kept silent and was alone, I said, 'I urge you by the Truth and the Truth, tell me a Hadith you heard from Allah's Messenger ﷺ that you have understood and are familiar with.' Abu Hurayrah said: 'I will do so; I will narrate a Hadith to you, narrated to me by Allah's Messenger ﷺ and which I was taught.'

Then Abu Hurayrah lost consciousness for a while. He became conscious again and said, 'I will narrate a Hadith to you, narrated to me by Allah's Messenger ﷺ in this house while no one else was with us except him and I.' Then, Abu Hurayrah went unconscious again for a while. He regained consciousness and wiped his face and said: 'I will do so; I will tell you a Hadith, narrated to me by Allah's Messenger ﷺ while him and I were in this house, none was with us except him and I.'

Then, Abu Hurayrah lost consciousness again and then weakly wiped his face. I made him lean upright. When he recovered consciousness, he said, "Allah's Messenger ﷺ narrated to me that, 'On the Day of Resurrection, Allah the Mighty and Sublime will descend to the servants to judge between them, and each nation will be humbled to their knees.

The first of those who will be called is a man who memorized the Qur'aan and a man who fights in the cause of Allah and a very wealthy man. So, He will ask the reciter (of the Qur'aan), 'Did I not grant you the knowledge of what I sent to My Messenger?' He will say, 'Yes, O Lord.' He will say, 'What did you follow of what you knew?' He will say, 'I used to recite it during the night and day prayers.' So, Allah will say to him, 'You lied' and the angels will say, 'You lied.' Allah will say, 'Rather, you wanted it to be said, So-and-so is a recite. And it has been said!'

The wealthy man will be brought and Allah will say, 'Did I not enrich you such that I made you not in need of anyone?' He will say, 'Yes.' He will say, 'How did you spend what I bestowed on you?' He will say: 'I used to maintain the ties of kinship and give charity.' Allah will say, "You lied' and the angels will say, 'You lied.' Allah will then say, 'Rather, you wanted it to be said: so-and–so is generous. And that has been said.'

The one who was killed in the cause of Allah will be brought and it will be said to him, 'In what situation were you killed?' He will say, 'You commanded me to fight in your cause, and

I fought until I was killed.' Allah will say, 'You lied', and the angels will say, 'You lied.' And Allah – the Mighty and Sublime – will say to him, 'Rather, you wanted it to be said, so-and-so is brave; and that has been said.' Then, Allah's Messenger ﷺ tapped my knees and said, 'O Abu Hurayrah! Those three are the first creatures of Allah to be made fuel for the Fire on the Day of Resurrection!'"[106]

2. Sincerity Magnifies and Multiplies Deeds

That is owing to the fact that Allah the Mighty and Sublime multiplies it and rewards the sincere in his deeds by multiplying his actions and magnifying them such that he will find it on the Day of Resurrection, much more than he expected. The great Imam, Abdullah bin Al-Mubarak[107] said, "Many a simple good deed is multiplied by the intention; and many a great deed is made insignificant by the intention."[108]

One of the pious wrote to his friend, "Make the intentions for your deeds pure and few of the deeds will suffice you."[109]

---

106 Reported by Imam Ibn Khuzaymah in his *Sahih*, the Book on *Zakaah*: The Chapter on Being Stern on Giving Charity for Show-Off and Fame: 4/115, 116 with a chain of transmission whose narrators are reliable as mentioned by the editor. In *At-Targeeb wat-Tarheeb*: 1/64, an addition occurs at the end of the Hadith that a man entered upon Mu'aawiyah and told him about the Hadith and Mu'aawiyah said: 'This had been done to those; how about those remaining amongst the people?' Then, Mu'aawiyah wept profusely until we thought he would die. Then we said: 'This man has brought an evil; then Mu'aawiyah got conscious and said: 'Allah and His Messenger said the truth: **"They are those for whom there is nothing in the Hereafter but Fire; and vain are the deeds they did therein. And of no effect is that which they used to do."**

107 He died in the year 181 AH. See: *Nuzhat ul-Fudalaa*: 2/654.

108 *Nuzhat ul-Fudalaa*: 2/657.

109 *Ithaaf us-Saadat il-Muttaqeen*: by Az-Zubaydee: 13/87.

3. Sincerity Purifies the Heart from Filth

Because the heart ever turns over and over, and is always busy; it turns away from goodness with the slightest confusion. But sincerity ensures that the heart is purified and turns it towards its Lord. The Prophet ﷺ said, "Three things do not leave rancor in the Muslim's heart: Making actions sincere for Allah, giving good advice to the leaders and sticking to the group of the Muslims because their supplications reach those behind them."[110]

The meaning of, "...do not leave rancor in the Muslim's heart..." is that, it does not allow rancor to remain in it or that the heart does not harbor rancor together with these three traits.[111]

Imam Makhul[112] رحمه الله said, "When a servant is sincere for forty days the fountains of wisdom outpour to his tongue from his heart."[113] Abu Sulayman Ad-Daaraanee[114] رضي الله عنه said, "When a servant is sincere, much of obsession and show-off goes off him."[115]

4. It Guarantees Steadfastness upon Good Deeds

So, "sincerity grants the servant the strength of continuity because the one who acts for the sake of the people and the one who acts for the cravings of the belly or lust soon stops when he does not get what satisfies his appetite. Similarly,

110 Reported by a number of the scholars with chains that strengthen one another, see: *Majma'u uz-Zawaaid*: 1/142-144.

111 *Tahdheeb Madaarij is-Saalikeen*: pg 321.

112 Abu Muslim Ad-Dimashqee, the ascetic and *Taabi'ee*. He died around 112 AH. See *Siyar A'alaam in-Nubalaa*: 5/155-160.

113 *Tahdheeb Madaarij is-Saalikeen*: pg 322.

114 A great Imam, an ascetic – Abdur-Rahmaan bin Ahmad Al-'Ansee Ad-Daaraanee. He died in the year 215 AH. See *Siyar A'alaam in-Nubalaa*: 1/182-186.

115 *Tahdheeb Madaarij is-Saalikeen*: pg 322.

the one who does good deeds for fame drops and slackens when it becomes clear to him that his expectations are not attainable. The one who acts seeking the pleasure of a leader or head also stops or lags when the leader is removed or the head dies.

As for the one who acts for the sake of Allah, he neither stops nor gives up, nor slackens, because the One for whose sake he acts is ever present and never ceases to exist. The Face of Allah is everlasting when the faces of the people will cease to exist…Hence the pious say: What is for Allah endures and continues; but what is for other than Allah ceases and breaks. And this is what occurs in reality, and what we have seen, perceived and continue to see and observe in every time and place."[116]

5. Sincerity Transforms Permissible Actions to the Level of Worship

Sincerity is the panacea of deeds which when placed on any deed – even when the deed is from the ordinarily permissible matters and mere value of a group of people – converts it to an act of worship and closeness to Allah (the Exalted)…

Regarding those who fight in His cause, Allah – the most High – said:

.... ذَٰلِكَ بِأَنَّهُمۡ لَا يُصِيبُهُمۡ ظَمَأٞ وَلَا نَصَبٞ وَلَا مَخۡمَصَةٞ فِي سَبِيلِ ٱللَّهِ وَلَا
يَطَـُٔونَ مَوۡطِئٗا يَغِيظُ ٱلۡكُفَّارَ وَلَا يَنَالُونَ مِنۡ عَدُوّٖ نَّيۡلًا إِلَّا كُتِبَ لَهُم بِهِۦ عَمَلٞ
صَٰلِحٌۚ إِنَّ ٱللَّهَ لَا يُضِيعُ أَجۡرَ ٱلۡمُحۡسِنِينَ ١٢٠ وَلَا يُنفِقُونَ نَفَقَةٗ صَغِيرَةٗ

116 *An-Niyyah wal-Ikhlaas*: Dr. Yusuf Al-Qaradawi: 103, 104.

وَلَا كَبِيرَةً وَلَا يَقْطَعُونَ وَادِيًا إِلَّا كُتِبَ لَهُمْ لِيَجْزِيَهُمُ ٱللَّهُ أَحْسَنَ مَا كَانُوا۟ يَعْمَلُونَ ﴿١٢١﴾

«That is because they suffer neither thirst nor fatigue, nor hunger in the Cause of Allah, nor they take any step to raise the anger of disbelievers nor inflict any injury upon an enemy but is written to their credit as a deed of righteousness. Surely, Allah wastes not the reward of the *Muhsinun*. Nor do they spend anything (in Allah's Cause) - small or great - nor cross a valley, but is written to their credit, that Allah may recompense them with the best of what they used to do (i.e. Allah will reward their good deeds according to the reward of their best deeds which they did in the most perfect manner).»

At-Tawbah (Q9:120-121)

So, He made their hunger, thirst, the steps they take and what they spend to be put down for them in their record of goodness with Allah the Mighty and Sublime as long as it was was in the cause of Allah. Abu Hurayrah ﵁ reported that the Prophet ﷺ said: "Whoever prepares a horse for the cause of Allah, out of faith in Allah and in affirmation of His promise, its feeding and drinking, and its feaces and urine are to his credit on the Day of Resurrection".[117] [118]

6. It is the means of gaining Allah's Company and Help

Allah the Mighty and Sublime said regarding the

117 Reported by Imam Al-Bukhaari in his *Sahih*: The Book of Jihad: The Chapter On Whoever Prepares a Horse based on His saying: **"...including steeds of war..."** 4/34.

118 *An-Niyyat Wal-Iklhaas*: 104, 105.

companions who witnessed the *Ba'at ur-Ridwaan* (Pledge of Favour) under the tree:

لَّقَدْ رَضِيَ ٱللَّهُ عَنِ ٱلْمُؤْمِنِينَ إِذْ يُبَايِعُونَكَ تَحْتَ ٱلشَّجَرَةِ فَعَلِمَ مَا فِي قُلُوبِهِمْ فَأَنزَلَ ٱلسَّكِينَةَ عَلَيْهِمْ وَأَثَـٰبَهُمْ فَتْحًا قَرِيبًا ﴿١٨﴾

«Indeed, Allah was pleased with the believers when they gave their *Ba'ah* (pledge) to you (O Muhammad ﷺ) under the tree, He knew what was in their hearts, and He sent down As-*Sakinah* (calmness and tranquillity) upon them, and He rewarded them with a near victory.»

Al-Fath (Q48:18)

The leader of the Muslims, Umar, wrote to Abu Musah Al-'Ash'aree رضي الله عنه whom he made the governor of Basra: "Whoever makes his intention sincere, Allah will suffice him regarding that between himself and the people; but whoever only puts up goodness for the sake of the people, Allah knows it from his heart and disgraces him…"[119]

7.4 Manifestations of Complete Absence of Sincerity or Its Mix-Up

Imam Al-Ghazali رحمه الله mentioned some manifestations of the absence of sincerity or its mix-up - its being marred by matters suspended in the mind – since it affects many, is hidden and because the one who is affected may think that he is from the righteous! So, he said:

119 *Ithaaf us-Saadat il-Muttaqeen*: 13/87, and Az-Zubaydee referred the narration to *Al-Hilyah* of Abu Nu'aym.

> "We will now talk about a person who is motivated by nearness (to Allah) but something else such as show-off or other things from the desires of the heart mix-up with this original intention. For example, the servant may fast to benefit from the enthusiasm that comes from fasting while still intending closeness to Allah. Or he may free a slave to be free from his maintenance and bad character. Or he can perform the pilgrimage to better his humour from the journey and get free from an evil that could afflict him in his city or run-away from an enemy of his in his house. He might also go because he is bored of his household or a particular job he had been busy with off which he likes some days.

A person may also fight (in a *Jihad*) against the enemy to perfect warfare, learn the use of armory so that he is to prepare the forces and march them. He can also pray in the late-night while intending to drive away doze and keep watch over his household and beasts. Likewise, he may acquire knowledge to easily get sufficient wealth or become honoured among the kinsfolk or so that his estate and money is protected from being coveted because of the honour attached to knowledge.

He can get busy with teaching and admonishing to get rid of the agony of quietness or relax with the delight of prophetic narrations. He might get busy with serving the scholars or the Sufis (!) to gain honour amongst the people or followership in this world. Such may hand-write a copy of the Qur'aan to better his writing from regularly writing. He can perform the ablution just to get clean or ease off (from severe dryness).

He could narrate Hadith to be known to have *'Uluww al-*

Isnaad (high-level chain of transmission) or fast to ease himself of the burdens of regular cooking or to be able to completely face his engagements so that food does not form a distraction. Such may visit the sick so that he will be visited when sick or witness burial rites so that the burial rites of his household can also be attended or do something like that in order to be known for goodness, mentioned for it and looked at as a pious and dignified person.

In any case, his original intention is to seek closeness to Allah (the Exalted), but he added one of these serious matters until the action became less significant and lost perfect sincerity...

In a nutshell, when any kind of worldly matter in which the soul finds rest and to which the heart inclines - whether simple or great -, infiltrates the action, it stains its purity and removes its sincerity. Yet, man is enmeshed in these affairs and plunged in his desires. Hardly is any of his deeds and worship free from matters or worldly targets of these kinds. As such, it is said: 'whoever submits in his life-time sincerely, seeking the Face of Allah (the Exalted) for a moment will succeed.' This is owing to the importance of sincerity and the difficulty in the purification of the heart from these stains."[120]

From the manifestations of mixed-up sincerity also, is that "the praying person, no matter how sincere he is in his prayer, when he is been looked at by a group of people or a person comes in to him; he says (to himself): 'Make your prayer nice so that this person present gives you dignifying and pious look and does not look down upon you or back-bite

120 *Ithaaf us-Saadat il-Muttaqeen*: 13/93-95. And the solution to these difficulties on the matters of sincerity will be mentioned in the subsequent pages – Allah willing.

you.' So, his limbs are in reverence, his appendages tranquil and he betters the prayer!"[121]

There is yet another manifestation, more subtle and obscure in the matters of sincerity wherein the praying person continues in his prayer and does not give attention to the *Shaytaan* and his delusions. So, he comes from another angle and says to him: "You are one that is followed, taken after and looked at. What you do is narrated and others follow you; so you have the reward of their deeds if you do the deeds well and you carry the blame if you do it badly. So, beautify your deeds before him perhaps he follows you in reverence and bettering worship."[122]

This is a good aim; but if the praying person is in secret, he does not put in reverence and nice worship, then those actions of his when he is amongst the people is also from the delusions of the *Shaytaan* and his deceptions. There is still another more subtle and obscure manifestation; and that is, that "the praying-person recognizes that from sincerity is that his worship in secret is as that he does amongst the people and he is shy towards himself and his Lord to show reverence before His creatures more than he is used to. So, he betters his worship in secret as he does in the sight of the people and prays amongst the people too like that. This is also from concealed show-off because he bettered his prayers in the secret so that he could also better it in the sight of the people and he would not have differentiated between both. Thus, his attention is to the creatures both in the secret and in the open. But sincerity is that the witnessing of the beasts and that of the people should be uniform."[123]

Another level, more obscure and pernicious is when the

121 *Ithaaf us-Saadat il-Muttaqeen*: 13/107-110.

122 The previous reference.

123 The previous reference.

Shaytaan says to the praying person while amongst the people, "contemplate the greatness of Allah and His Sublimity and the One before whom you stand and be shy of Allah's looking at your heart while it is heedless of Him. As a result, his heart becomes heedful, his limbs are filled with reverence and he thinks that that is real sincerity. But this is no other than deception and folly because if his reverence were owing to contemplation of His Sublimity, this thought will always be with him even in the secret."[124]

This form may be unknown to the servant and so, the *Shaytaan* destroys his sincerity – And there is no power or might but by Allah, the most High, the Great. "No one is safe from the *Shaytaan* except the one that gives thorough consideration to affairs and becomes successful out of Allah's protection, success and guidance. Else, the *Shaytaan* is ever with those given to the worship of Allah. He does not become unaware of them for any moment so that he could make them show-off in every movement, even in lining the eyes, shortening the moustache, perfuming on Friday and wearing the clothes."[125]

7.5 Foundations and Words of Caution

1. Difficulty of establishing perfect sincerity

Perfect sincerity should not be ideated except for the one deep in love for Allah the Mighty and Sublime and concerned about the hereafter. And that is because man forgets a great deal, greatly inclines to the worldly matters and is much deceived by it. Thus, the one in this condition,

124 The previous reference.

125 The previous reference.And the solution to these difficulties on the matters of sincerity will be mentioned in the subsequent pages – Allah willing.

perfect sincerity should not be conceived of him except the one from those Allah (the Exalted) has granted success.

This is because who amongst us – for example – does not feel appetite for food for its being food, or even, because it makes him strong to worship Allah? Who amongst us sleeps to get strong to worship Allah (the Exalted)? Who fulfills evacuates his bowels so that it assists him to free his mind from attachment with the worldly affairs and better his connection with Allah the Mighty and Sublime? And so on.

Therefore, the servant has to be upright and precise, concentrate on the attainment of perfect sincerity and not turn to the dangerous and destructive delusions of the *Shaytaan* in this regard. Likewise, one should not take it lightly if his righteous deeds mix-up while he is capable of purifying it from the ailments that destroy deeds and take away its benefits.

2. Not leaving good deeds for fear of mixed-up intentions

Abu Taalib Al-Maakee[126] رحمه الله said: "The servant should not give up a good deed fearing its infiltration by a failure for that is what his enemy desires of him. Rather, he should be upon his original intention of pure sincerity. If it (i.e. the intention) is infiltrated, he should place cure on it and try to reject and remove it remaining steadfast upon his good intention and character. He should not leave any deed for the sake of the people, being shy of them, and in detestation of their considering him virtuous; for acting for the sake of the people is *Shirk* (ascription of partners to Allah) and abandoning it for their sake is show-off. Leaving a good

---

126 Muhammad bin 'Ali bin 'Atiyyah Al-Haarithee, the Imam and ascetic; he died in the year 386 AH. See *Siyar A'alaam in-Nubalaa*: 16/536–537.

deed for the fear of the infiltration of a failure is of ignorance and leaving it when the ailment has crept into it is weakness and frailty. Whoever commences a deed for the sake of Allah (the Exalted) and comes out of it for His sake, what comes between that will not harm him after rejecting and not accommodating it."[127]

3. The Intention can be rectified after its corruption

Some of the people may think that if an action is started with a bad intention, then it is obligatory to abandon it and not continue with it. But the truth is that, the intention can be rectified while the action can be continued and not abandoned. Some of the pious predecessors used to commence seeking for knowledge while not having perfect sincerity, then, they took heed and returned to Allah, rectified their intentions and carried on with the search for knowledge with the right intention.

Imam Adh-Dhahabee (d. 748) ﵀ said, "Abdur-Razzaaq (d. 211) said: Ma'mar (d. 154) told us that: 'It used to be said: A person searches for knowledge for other than Allah and the knowledge holds him back from that so that it becomes for Allah'.

I say: Yes, he started seeking for it, spurred by the love for knowledge, passion to take out ignorance from himself, the love for work and things like that. He did not realize the obligation of sincerity or the right intention regarding it. So, when he realized, he cautioned himself and feared the perils of his original intention and then, the right intention completely or partially comes to him. He may even turn in repentance from the wrong intention and regret known through his reducing claims and love for disputation.

127 *Ithaaf us-Saadat il-Muttaqeen*: 13/105.

Whoever intends to increase in his knowledge and is self-conceited, if he boasts about his knowledge or says: I am more learned than so-and-so, then away with him!"[128]

Imam Adh-Dhahabee said elsewhere, "The pious predecessors used to seek knowledge for the sake of Allah, so they attained nobility and became model leaders. Some of them sought it not for the sake of Allah at the beginning. They achieved it, became very learned and cautioned their souls; knowledge made them gain sincerity on the way as Mujaahid (d. 101) and others said: 'We searched for this knowledge while not having much of (the right) intention, and then, Allah granted the right intention later."[129]

4. Taints of sincerity affect reward but do not completely invalidate it

This is because whoever seeks the Face of Allah (the Exalted) through an action and is sincere in it but a worldly affair taints it unknowingly or out of the over-bearing effect of desire, the reward of the deed is not completely rendered vain – as a mercy and blessing from Allah. "We seek refuge with Allah that the affair should be like that,[130] for this is difficulty in the world and a means for the Muslims to despair since one may not be completely free from the likes of these taints except in few cases. Thus, the effect of such is reduction in reward but that it is completely rendered useless, no."

Therefore, it is necessary for the servant "to ever be – after much effort – between criticism and acceptance, fearing that there is any failure in his worship whose punishment

---

128 *Nuzhat ul-Fudalaa*: 2/560.

129 The previous reference.

130 That any action into which insincerity infiltrates should be completely vain. (TN)

is greater than its reward. This was the way of the fearful servants from the people of deep thought and contemplation and that is how every deep-thinking person should be."[131]

5. The permissibility of showing some good deeds for good intention

Basically good deeds should concealed and not made known to anyone except if it is from those deeds that are necessarily shown like the pilgrimage, the prayers in congregation for example. However, some good deeds performed in the secret could be shown and spoken about if two things happen to the servant:

The First: safety from show-off.

The Other: Having to achieve a religious benefit by making the pious deed known like the weak's following the strong or calming down the people and giving them glad tidings. An example of it is what Abu Sufyaan bin Al-Haarith رضي الله عنه the cousin of the Prophet ﷺ said to his household at the point of death, "Do not cry over me for I never committed any sin since I accepted Islam."[132]

7.6 Signs of Sincerity

The sincere one has signs with which he is known such as: fear of popularity, charging the soul with negligence and slackness, acting in silence, not seeking praise and commendation or being deceived by it, not refusing to commend the one who deserves to be commended and praised with its etiquettes. For such, the action is same to

131 *Ithaaf us-Saadat il-Muttaqeen*; 13/120.
132 The previous reference: 10/162.

him - for the sake of Allah - whether he is in control or controlled.

Likewise being joyful at the pleasure of Allah and not that of the people, making his pleasure and displeasure for the sake of Allah and not himself, being patient over the lengthiness of the path of the legal responsibilities and delayed help, glad with the successes of his fellows or at least not geting unhappy about that. He would also make efforts at the rectification of his hidden from self-conceit, not vindicating himself, concealing his acts of obedience except for a clear pressing benefit, and others amongst the signs.

Each of what has been mentioned has examples, supporting proofs and lengthy explanations, which I have not mentioned for brevity.[133]

Things that Help on Sincerity

1. Supplication and Turning to Allah (the Exalted)

Since He is the One that assists and who is turned to in every matter – Glorious is He and Exalted.

2. Knowledge

That is, that the servant recognizes the importance of sincerity and understand the methods of the *Shaytaan* and his attempts at the soul. He should also know what is in the Book of Allah (the Exalted) and the *Sunnah* of Allah's Messenger ﷺ of encouragement towards sincerity some of which had been mentioned.

133 Regarding what has been mentioned, see: *An-Niyyat wal-Ikhlaas* by Dr. Yusuf Al-Qaradawi: 69-94.

3. Making Efforts

Allah (the Exalted) said:

وَٱلَّذِينَ جَٰهَدُوا۟ فِينَا لَنَهْدِيَنَّهُمْ سُبُلَنَا ۚ وَإِنَّ ٱللَّهَ لَمَعَ ٱلْمُحْسِنِينَ ﴿٦٩﴾

«As for those who strive hard in Us (Our Cause), We will surely guide them to Our Paths (i.e. Allah's Religion - Islamic Monotheism). And verily, Allah is with the Muhsinun (good doers).»

Al-'Ankabut (Q29:69)

4. Companionship with the Sincere Ones

For that brings about the love for sincerity and acting to become used to it. Knowing about their efforts in this regard is really very beneficial.

5. Reading the biographies of the Salaf and those after them amongst the pious

Nothing is most beneficial – after Allah's granting success –as studying the biographies of the pious predecessors, their beneficial sayings and their great efforts.

Each of these has lengthy explanations, examples and corroborating proofs which I left for brevity.[134]

134 Regarding what has been mentioned, see: *An-Niyyat wal-Ikhlaas* by Dr. Yusuf Al-Qaradawi: 69-94.

Chapter 8
At-Tawbah (Repentance)

It is the first level of the turners to Allah (the Exalted) and the rectifiers of their affairs with Him, "and the beginning of the path of the devout servants, the stronghold of the successful, the first bold venture of the Followers (of the righteous), the key to the steadfastness of the Incliners (to good deeds) and the point of choice and selection of the close servants."[135]

"Repentance is the first level, its mid and its last. The striving servant does not leave it, he continues upon it until death."[136]

Allah the Mighty and Sublime has exhorted regarding it in many places in His Book:

يَٰٓأَيُّهَا ٱلَّذِينَ ءَامَنُواْ تُوبُوٓاْ إِلَى ٱللَّهِ تَوۡبَةٗ نَّصُوحًا عَسَىٰ رَبُّكُمۡ أَن يُكَفِّرَ عَنكُمۡ
سَيِّـَٔاتِكُمۡ وَيُدۡخِلَكُمۡ جَنَّٰتٖ تَجۡرِي مِن تَحۡتِهَا ٱلۡأَنۡهَٰرُ .... ﴿٨﴾

«O you who believe! Turn to Allah with sincere repentance! It may be that your Lord will remit from

135 *Ithaaf us-Saadat il-Muttaqeen*: 10/ 547.
136 *Tahdheeb Madaarij is-Saalikeen*: pg 121

you your sins, and admit you into Gardens under which rivers flow (Paradise)...»

At-Tahrim (Q66:8).

He has described Himself as One who greatly overlooks for those who repent. He (the Exalted) said:

وَإِنِّي لَغَفَّارٌ لِّمَن تَابَ وَءَامَنَ وَعَمِلَ صَٰلِحًا ثُمَّ ٱهْتَدَىٰ ﴿٨٢﴾

«And verily, I am indeed Forgiving to him who repents, believes (in My Oneness, and associates none in worship with Me) and does righteous good deeds, and then remains constant in doing them, (till his death).»

Taha (Q20:82)

He the Sublime also said:

.... إِنَّ ٱللَّهَ هُوَ ٱلتَّوَّابُ ٱلرَّحِيمُ ﴿١١٨﴾

«Verily, Allah is the One Who accepts repentance, Most Merciful.»

At-Tawbah (Q9:118)

Allah (the Exalted) is happy at the repentance of His servant, even when He the Mighty and Sublime said:

.... إِنَّ ٱللَّهَ لَغَنِيٌّ عَنِ ٱلْعَٰلَمِينَ ﴿٦﴾

«Verily, Allah is free of all wants from the 'Alameen (mankind, jinns, and all that exists).»

Al-Ankabut:(Q29:6)

And that: "If the first of you and the last of you, the men of you and the Jinn of you were to have the most pious heart as a single man amongst you; that will not increase anything in My dominion. And if the first of you and the last of you, and the men amongst you and the Jinn amongst you have the most evil heart as that of any single one of you, that will not reduce anything in My dominion."[137] Yet, He – Glorious is He - is happy at the repentance of His servant out of His Generosity and Favour.

The Messenger of Allah ﷺ has depicted that in the best form. He ﷺ said, "Allah is more joyous for the repentance of His servant when he turns to Him than one of you who was on his ridding camel in the desert and he missed it while it was carrying his food and drink. He lost all hopes of finding it. Then, he went to recline under a tree waiting, having lost any hope of finding it. All of a sudden, he saw the noseband of his camel tied to the tree. While in this condition, it was standing by it (the tree), so, he took hold of the noseband and then said out of overwhelming joy: 'O Allah, You are my servant, and I am Your Lord.' He erred out of very great joy."[138]

Imam Ibn al-Qayyim had given extensive explanations on the reason for the joy which is that Allah (the Exalted) is Generous, Beneficent and Kind while the sinning servant is vulnerable to Allah's anger, wrath and retribution. His anger

137 Reported by Muslim in his *Sahih*: the Book on Righteousness and Relations and Manners; The Chapter on The prohibition of Injustice: 16/106.

138 Reported by Imam Muslim in his *Sahih*: The Book on Repentance: The Chapter on Exhortation Towards Repentance and Joy Through It: 17/220.

and wrath could replace His pleasure, and His retribution and punishment may substitute His generosity, kindness and favour. So, his disobedience to Him brings about Allah's actions which other than it are more beloved to Him and contradict the generosity and beneficence that is usual with His Essence. Thus, when the servant turns to his Lord, Allah is joyous by the return of the generosity, beneficence and kindness to His servant.

There is another significance of Allah's Joy and it is that Allah created the creatures to worship and obey Him. So, if the servant leaves obedience and servitude which the purpose of his been created, he has left the most beloved thing to Allah and the reason for creation. If the servant returns to this objective which is the most beloved thing to Allah, his Creator and Originator, Allah's love for him becomes stronger. This is the import of the statement of Ibn al-Qayyim رحمه الله.

He رحمه الله has also mentioned a narration which explains the condition of the repenting servant with Allah – and to Allah belongs the best description. He said: "One of the devout mentioned that he saw a door opened on a road and a child came out of it calling for help and crying. His mother was behind him driving him away until he came out. She closed the door to his face and entered. The child went nearby and started thinking but could neither find a resort except the home from which he was evicted nor anyone to accommodate him except his mother.

So, he returned with broken heart, sad, and found the door locked. He rested on it, placed his cheek on the door step and slept. When his mother came out and found him in that condition, she held him to herself, kissed him and wept, saying, 'O my son, where did you go? Who will take care of you besides me? Did I not warn you not to disobey me and not make me contradict innately showing you mercy, kindness and liking good for you through your disobeying me?' Then, she took him and went in.

Ponder over this saying of the mother: "…do not make me contradict innately showing you mercy, kindness and liking good for you through your disobeying me" and his saying "Allah is more merciful to His servants than the mother to her child."[139] Can the mercy of the mother ever be compared with Allah's Mercy which encompasses all things?

Allah (the Exalted) loves the repenting servant. He said:

... إِنَّ ٱللَّهَ يُحِبُّ ٱلتَّوَّٰبِينَ ... ﴿٢٢٢﴾

«Truly, Allah loves those who turn unto Him in repentance»

Al-Baqarah (Q2:222)

The Prophet ﷺ had said, "Certainly, Allah – the Mighty and Sublime – stretches His Hand in the night for the one who sinned in the day to turn in repentance, and stretches his hand in the day that the one who sinned in the night may turn in repentance. (This will continue) until the sun rises from its place of set."[140]

The chosen one ﷺ regularly turns in repentance and urges his companions upon same. He ﷺ said, "O people! Turn

139 Reported by Imam Muslim in the Book On Repentance: the Chapter On The Limitlessness of Allah's Mercy And that It Surpasses His Anger: 17/226 and its wording is: "than this (woman) with her child".

140 Reported by Imam Muslim in his *Sahih*: The Book on Repentance: The Chapter on The Acceptance of Repentance from Sin even when it Reoccurs: 17/231.

in repentance to Allah, for I turn in repentance to Him a hundred times daily."[141] The pious predecessors earnestly recommended turning in repentance to Allah in many narrations from which is what Talq bin Hubayb[142] ﵀ said, "The rights of Allah are greater than the servant keeping them; but you should wake up repenting and spend the evening repenting."[143]

8.1 The Meaning of Repentance and Its Ruling

At-Tawbah: Turning away from sin.

And it is said: "It is turning away from what Allah dislikes openly and secretly towards what he likes openly and secretly."[144]

At-Tawbah (Repentance) is obligatory immediately from every sin. Allah (the Exalted) said:

.... وَتُوبُوٓا۟ إِلَى ٱللَّهِ جَمِيعًا أَيُّهَ ٱلْمُؤْمِنُونَ لَعَلَّكُمْ تُفْلِحُونَ ﴿٣١﴾

«And all of you beg Allah to forgive you all, O believers, that you may be successful»

An-Nur (Q24:31)

Therefore, "hastening towards repentance from sin is an

141 Reported by Imam Muslim in his *Sahih*: The Book on Remembrance, Supplication, Repentance, and Forgiveness: The Chapter on Repentance: 17/191.

142 Basree, ascetic, and from the eminent scholars; he died in the year 100 AH. See: *Nuzhat ul-Fudalaa*: 1/455.

143 *Ithaaf us-Saadat il-Muttaqeen*: 1/603.

144 *Tahdheeb Madaarij is-Saalikeen*: pg. 176.

immediate obligation and it is not permissible to delay it. When one delays it, he sins by his delaying it. When he repents from the sin, it will remain that he repents from another sin, which is the repentance from delaying repentance. Only in few cases does this come up the mind of the repenting servant; rather, in his view, if he repents from a sin nothing is left upon him while repentance for the delay of repentance actually is left on him."[145],[146]

8.2 The Levels of Sins

Sins are of two levels: Major and Minor.

Some of the scholars do not veiw this classification correct; they rather consider every act of disobedience to Allah a major sin. And that is because sining is being fearless and daring towards Allah (the Exalted), and owing to their considering the greatness of Allah's rights over His servants. Some others amongst the scholars say: It is only said to be minor vis-à-vis the one worse than it; else, every sin is major.[147] However, this is the weaker of the opinions because Allah (the Exalted) classed sins into great, major sins and faults, minor sins.

He the Mighty and Sublime said:

ٱلَّذِينَ يَجْتَنِبُونَ كَبَٰٓئِرَ ٱلْإِثْمِ وَٱلْفَوَٰحِشَ إِلَّا ٱللَّمَمَ .... ﴿٣٤﴾

145 *Tahdheeb Madaarij is-Saalikeen*: pg. 157.
146 See: *Ithaaf us-Saadat il-Muttaqeen*: 10/612.
147 See *Ithaaf us-Saadat il-Muttaqeen*: pg 157.

«Those who avoid great sins except the small faults»

An-Najm (Q53:32)

And the truth – And Allah knows best - is that, sins are classified into major and minor. The major sins are not restricted to any specific number, rather, everything that Allah prohibits, threatening fire as punishment for it or His anger or wrath or punishment or for which He obligates Legal punishment in this world for the offender is a major sin. The minor sins are other than these.[148]

Minor Sins Could Turn into Major Sins

Ibn al-Qayyim mentioned that: "The Major sin could be accompanied with shyness, fear and exaggeration and it becomes like the Minor sins, and a Minor sin could be accompanied by little shyness, undauntedness, fearlessness and belittling and it becomes like Major sin. Even, it could make it be at the greatest level."[149] As such, a Minor sin could change to a major sin and that is due to causes – in addition to what Ibn ul-Qayyim stated -:

1. Persistence and Continuity upon Minor Sin

This brings about hard-heartedness and the heart being sealed. Thus, it is said, "Sins are neither considered small with persistence nor great with repentance."[150]

148 *Ithaaf us-Saadat il-Muttaqeen*: 1/615, 616 with slight modification. There are other statements regarding the definition of the major sins which I have left for brevity. You can refer to them in the reference given.

149 *Tahdheeb Madaarij is-Saalikeen*: pg 185, 186.

150 This saying is attributed to Ibn Abbas in narrations (with chains), that strengthen one another. See: *Ithaaf us-Saadat il-Muttaqeen*: 10/687.

2. Belittling Sins

The Prophet ﷺ said, “Beware of the destroyer-sins, for they assemble on a person until they destroy him… “[151] Ibn Mas’ud رضي الله عنه said: “The believer considers his sins as if he sat at the foot of a mountain fearing that it falls on him. But the sinful person sees his sins as flies around his nose and so, does like this”. Ibn Shihaab then moved his hand above his nose.[152]

One of the pious predecessors said: “The sin for which forgiveness is not (usually) sought is that regarding which the servant says: ‘I wish every sin that I commit is like this.’”[153] That is, that he considers it insignificant. As such, Anas bin Maalik رضي الله عنه said to some of the *Taabi’een*, “If you know any deed more insignificant in your sight than the hair; we used to consider it (the deed) at the time of the Prophet ﷺ from the destroyer-sins.”[154]

Anas رضي الله عنه did not mean to say that the Major sins were considered Minor after Allah’s Messenger ﷺ but he only said that because, “the companions’ knowledge of the greatness of Allah is more perfect. Hence to them, the minor sins, together with Allah’s Mightiness is Major. So, what is considered significant from a learned is not considered such from an ignorant person and the layman is forgiven regarding some matters while the learned is not forgiven of its kind; because sins and acts of disobedience become

---

151 Imam Al-Haythamee said in *Majmau’ uz-Zawaaid*: 10/192: Reported by Ahmad and At-Tabaraanee in *Al-Awsat* and the narrators of both chains are trustworthy asides ‘Imran bin Daawir Al-Qattaan and he had been declared reliable.

152 That is, he gestured towards his nose with his hands to drive away the fly, as is explained by Ibn Shihaab Az-Zuhree, the narrator of the Hadith.

153 *Ithaaf us-Saadat il-Muttaqeen*: 10/689.

154 Reported by Al-Bukhaari in his Sahih: The Book on Heart-Softeners: The Chapter on What Must be Avoided of Destroyer-Sins: 8/128.

more significant based on the knowledge of the person involved."[155]

Sins should necessarily be considered significant for "when they are belittled, one does not repent from them. The more it is considered significant so will the regret be upon committing them. The one who trivialize loss of some money – for example – he does not regret its loss, but when he realizes that it is a Dinar, his regret increases and its loss becomes more significant to him. Considering sins great comes from three things: taking the matter important, considering the Law-Giver great and truly affirming recompense."[156]

3. Being Joyful over Minor Sins:

So, the one who commits a minor sin, says for example: 'Do you not see how I disgraced so-and-so, and how I mentioned his shortcomings until I got him worried?' Or the transgressor says: 'if you saw how I beat so-and-so, and disgraced him'; and so on.

"Being careless about sins increase with more sins until such gets happy when he fulfils his forbidden desire. This joy he derives from sin, is evidence for his strong inclinations towards it, ignorance of the greatness of the One that is disobeyed and of its evil and the severity of its consequence. His being joyful over the sins covers all these and is more dangerous to him than the act itself...

So, when the negligence gets to this level, it gets him to – and necessarily so – the level of persistence (on the sin) which is continuous disobedience and strong zeal to repeat it which is itself, another sin, and is perhaps, more grievous

155 *Ithaaf us-Saadat il-Muttaqeen*: 10/690.
156 *Tahdheeb Madaarij is-Saalikeen*: pg. 124.

than the first sin. And that is from the evil consequence of sins: committing worse ones!"[157]

4. Taking Allah's Cover and Mercy for Granted

That is when the disobedient one becomes beguiled with Allah's covering over him and does not realize that it is respite from Allah. Even, he could think that Allah (the Exalted) loves him and favours him, as the Jews did by saying as told to us by Allah (the Exalted) from their stories:

نَحْنُ أَبْنَٰٓؤُاْ ٱللَّهِ وَأَحِبَّٰٓؤُهُۥۚ

«We are the children of Allah and His loved ones.»

Al-Ma'idah (Q5:18)

He the Mighty and Sublime also said:

.... وَيَقُولُونَ فِيٓ أَنفُسِهِمۡ لَوۡلَا يُعَذِّبُنَا ٱللَّهُ بِمَا نَقُولُۚ حَسۡبُهُمۡ جَهَنَّمُ يَصۡلَوۡنَهَاۖ فَبِئۡسَ ٱلۡمَصِيرُ ٨

«And they say within themselves: «Why should Allah punish us not for what we say?» Hell will be sufficient for them, they will burn therein, and worst indeed is that destination!»

Al-Mujadila (Q58:8)

5. Tearing Allah's Cover over Him by Mentioning Sins

So, whoever commits a minor sin and Allah covers him up,

157 *Tahdheeb Madaarij is-Saalikeen*: pg. 122, 123.

and then he shows it, mentioning and talking about it, he is multiplying his minor sin by what he adds to it. Some of the listeners may become interested in that sin which he committed; and he himself may make the listeners become interested and for this and other reasons, the Minor sins may become Major. The Prophet ﷺ said: "Everyone in my *Ummah* will be granted forgiveness except those who announce their sins. And from announcing sin is that a servant does something in the night and wakes up having been covered by his Lord; then he says: 'I did such-and-such yesterday.' He could also sleep having been covered by his Lord and he sleeps being covered but wakes up and removes Allah's cover over him."[158]

6. When the One who Commits a Minor Sin is Learned, Taken as a Model or One Known with Piety:

If such a person commits a minor sin knowingly and arrogantly out of making the texts appear supportive of his position; perhaps, that could have made it become Major. But whoever does that out of textual interpretation or due to annoyance or other than that, he may be forgiven especially if he has deeds that will necessitate that.

Ibn al-Qayyim رحمه الله said, "Also, the beloved and one with great righteous deeds may be forgiven what other than him may not be forgiven. He may be pardoned what other than him may not be pardoned. I heard *Shaykh al-Islam* Ibn Taimiyyah رحمه الله saying: 'Consider Musa – may the peace and blessings of Allah be upon him –, he threw the slates containing Allah's Words which He wrote with His Hand and broke it. He dragged the beard of another prophet like himself: Harun, slapped the angel of death and gouged out his eye, advised

158 Reported by Imam Muslim in his *Sahih*: The Book of Ascetism: The Chapter on the Prohibition of One's Tearing His Own Cover: 18/412.

His Lord on the Night of *Israa* about Muhammad ﷺ who has been raised over him. Yet his Lord tolerated all that for him, loves him and honours him for he stood for Allah in those serious conditions.

And consider Yunus bin Mutta who was not in those conditions in which Musa was, he was uncomfortable with his Lord once, so he imprisoned him in the belly of the fish. So in his case, he did not tolerate what He tolerated for Musa…Therefore, whoever has his good deeds greater than his sins will succeed and may not be punished and his sins will be forgiven him due to his good deeds.'"[159]

Conditions for Pardon of Major and Minor Sins

Repenting from minor sins has paths, such as:

1. Avoiding Major Sins

From the favours of Allah (the Exalted) on people is that He made keeping away from Major sins an automatic means of atonement for the Minor sins:

Allah (the Exalted) said:

إِن تَجْتَنِبُوا۟ كَبَآئِرَ مَا تُنْهَوْنَ عَنْهُ نُكَفِّرْ عَنكُمْ سَيِّـَٔاتِكُمْ وَنُدْخِلْكُم مُّدْخَلًا كَرِيمًا ﴿٣١﴾

«If you avoid the great sins which you are forbidden

159 *Tahdheeb Madaarij is-Saalikeen*: pg 186.

to do, We shall remit from you your (small) sins, and admit you to a Noble Entrance (i.e. Paradise).»

An-Nisa (Q4:31)

And the Prophet ﷺ said, "The five daily prayers, the Friday-prayer to another Friday-prayer, the Ramadan (Fasting) to another Ramadan (Fasting) are atonements for what is between them if the Major sins are avoided".[160]

2. Good Deeds

Whoever carries out good deeds, Minor sins will be atoned for him. For examples, the congregational prayer; it atones for Minor sins. The Prophet ﷺ said: "Whoever performs ablution for a prayer, perfects the ablution, and then goes to perform the obligatory prayer and prays it with the people or in congregation or in a mosque, his sins will be forgiven."[161]

3. Seeking Forgiveness

Abu Hurayrah رضي الله عنه narrated from the Prophet ﷺ from what he reports from his Lord the Mighty and Sublime and said, "My servant committed a sin and said, 'O Allah, forgive me my sins.'" Then He (the Exalted) said, "My servant committed a sin and recognized that he has a Lord who forgives sins and punishes due to sins." Then, he returns and commits a sin and then said: 'O my Lord, forgive me'". And He (the Exalted) said, "My servant committed a sin and recognized that he has a Lord who forgives sins and grabs due to sins. Thereafter, he returns and commits a sin and then said: 'O my Lord, forgive me.'" He (the Exalted) said, "My servant committed a sin and recognized that he has a

160 Reported by Imam Muslim: The Book on Purification: The Chapter on the Five Daily Prayers, the Friday-Prayer to another Friday-prayer Are Atonements for what comes between them: 3/470.

161 The previous reference.

Lord who forgives sins and grabs due to sins; do what you will for I have forgiven you."[162]

That is, as long as you sin and thereafter, turn in repentance, I will forgive you.

4. Saying the *Tasbeeh* and the Remembrance of Allah:

The Prophet ﷺ said: "Whoever says *Laa ilaaha illa Allah wahdahu laa shareekalah, lahul-Mulk wa lahul-Hamd wahuwa 'alaa kulli shay-in Qadeer* (There is no deity worthy of worship except Allah alone, He has no partner. His is the Dominion and Praise and He has power over all things) a hundred times on a day, he will have the reward of freeing ten slaves, a hundred virtues will be written for him, a hundred of his sins will be erased and it will be a protection for him against the *Shaytaan* on that day until evening. And no one does something better than this except one who does a deed better than that. And whoever says: *SubhaanAllah wabihamdihi* (Glorious is Allah and to Him is Praise) hundred times in a day, his sins will be removed even if they are like the foam of the sea."[163]

How to Repent from Major Sins

1. Regretting over the sin.
2. Abandoning it immediately.
3. Resolving not to return to it in the future.

From perfection of repentance is *Al-I'tidhaar* (expressing

---

162 The previous reference: The Book on Repentance: The Chapter on the Acceptance of Repentance even when it is Repeatedly: 17/230.

163 The previous reference: The Book On Remembrance, Supplication, Repentance, And Forgiveness: The Chapter On The Virtue Of the *Tahleel*, The *Tasbeeh* And Supplication: 17/186.

remorse) to Allah "and this does not mean *I'tidhaar* which is to make excuses for sins. It rather means saying in the heart and with the tongue (for example): 'O Allah, I am not innocent of any sin. So I express remorse. And I have no power so, I seek help. But I am guilty and I seek forgiveness. O Allah, I do not have any excuse, it is purely your right and my sin. So forgive me.'

Thus, it is an *I'tidhaar* (expression of remorse) by the showing weakness, humility and expressing regeret for being a victim of the over-bearing influence of the *Shaytaan*, the enemy, and the strength of the temptation of the Sin-Urging Soul.

And he should say with his tongue: 'O Lord, what I did was not out of belittling Your right or ignorance regarding You or disliking to obey You or taking Your warning lightly. It was from the over-bearing influence of the desire, the weakness to resist the sickness of desire and in expectation of your forgiveness, depending on Your pardon, thinking well of You, hoping for your favour and anticipating Your abundant beneficence and mercy. So, the deceiver swayed me regarding you; the Sin-Urging Soul, Your cover spread over me and my ignorance aided me. I have no resort except to you and no helper upon obeying You except through the success You grant.'

And things like this from sayings that contain appeal, want, recognition of weakness, and affirmation of servitude. This is from the perfection of repentance. Only those who cajole their Lord the Mighty and Sublime follow this path, and Allah loves that His servants to cajole Him."[164]

These conditions are suitable when the servant sins regarding something between himself and his Lord. But if the sin

164 *Tahdheeb Madaarij is-Saalikeen*: pg. 124.

is connected with the rights of the servants, two other conditions are attached to the three (mentioned above):

5. Seeking Freedom from the Servant and His Grievance.

That will be through fulfilling the right to the wronged person or "by seeking pardon from him after telling about it (i.e. the wrong) even if it is a right related to property or crime against his body or his heir as is authentically reported from the Prophet ﷺ that he said: 'Whoever usurps a right of his brother of wealth or honour should seek pardon for it today before there will be no *Dinar* or *Dirham* except good deeds and evil deeds.'[165]

But if the infringement is related to backbiting or slandering him, must he also tell him specifically and seek his pardon? Or he should only inform him that he has infringed his honour and may not necessarily specify it?[166] Or none of this or that is stipulated? Does it suffice that he turns to Allah for pardon without mentioning his slander or backbiting? There are three opinions regarding this."

Ibn al-Qayyim mentioned that the view of Ash-Shafi'i, Abu Hanifa and Maalik is that it is stipulated to tell him and seek his pardon. They derive evidence from crime against the body and the rights of wealth, both of which telling, seeking pardon and retribution is stipulated. But Ibn

165 Reported by Imam Al-Bukhaari in his *Sahih*: The Book on Infringement of Rights: The Chapter on the One who Infringes the Right of a Man and he Pardons Him; Should He tell Him of the Right? : 3/170. The wording of Al-Bukhaari is: "Whoever has infringed the right of anyone regarding his wealth or any other thing should seek his pardon today before there will be no *Dinar* or *Dirham*. If he has a good deed, it is taken away from him in the degree of his usurpation. And if he has no good deeds, some of the sins of his companion is taken and heaped on him."

166 That is, it is not preconditioned in repentance to specify how the honour was infringed, rather a general statement should be made.

Taimiyyah views that telling him should not bet stipulated for infringement on the honour of the wronged person or his being slandered and backbitten. His (i.e. the usurper's) repentance between himself and Allah suffices, and that the slanderer and backbiter says the opposite of what he had mentioned at the place (or to those to whom he said those things), and seek forgiveness for them. This is because the usurper's telling about the evil does not guarantee any benefit. It will only increase him (the offended) in hatred and grief while he could have been relaxed before hearing it. And the *Sharee'ah* will not permit something like this, how much more obligating it.

The difference between this situation – that is, the situation of slander and backbiting – and that of infringement on a person's body and property is that there is benefit in the two later ones considering the fact that the wronged person would benefit with the wealth (returned to him) and that if he (the usurper) tells what has happened to him, it will neither harm him, nor entail evil nor enmity. In fact, he may be happy with it as against telling him what will destroy his honour, day and night, of the various forms of defamation, backbiting, and slander."[167]

6. There is a Fifth condition Which is Very Important, and that is; that the Repentance Should be at its Time.

So, repentance will not be accepted from the servant at the point of death nor when the sun rises from its point of setting, at a time that Resurrection becomes certain. Allah (the Exalted) said:

167 *Tahdheeb Madaarij is-Saalikeen*: pg. 162, 163.

إِنَّمَا ٱلتَّوْبَةُ عَلَى ٱللَّهِ لِلَّذِينَ يَعْمَلُونَ ٱلسُّوٓءَ بِجَهَٰلَةٍ ثُمَّ يَتُوبُونَ مِن قَرِيبٍ
فَأُوْلَٰٓئِكَ يَتُوبُ ٱللَّهُ عَلَيْهِمْ ۗ وَكَانَ ٱللَّهُ عَلِيمًا حَكِيمًا ﴿١٧﴾ وَلَيْسَتِ ٱلتَّوْبَةُ لِلَّذِينَ
يَعْمَلُونَ ٱلسَّيِّـَٔاتِ حَتَّىٰٓ إِذَا حَضَرَ أَحَدَهُمُ ٱلْمَوْتُ قَالَ إِنِّى تُبْتُ ٱلْـَٰٔنَ وَلَا
ٱلَّذِينَ يَمُوتُونَ وَهُمْ كُفَّارٌ ۚ أُوْلَٰٓئِكَ أَعْتَدْنَا لَهُمْ عَذَابًا أَلِيمًا ﴿١٨﴾

«Allah accepts only the repentance of those who do evil in ignorance and foolishness and repent soon afterwards; it is they to whom Allah will forgive and Allah is Ever All-Knower, All-Wise. And of no effect is the repentance of those who continue to do evil deeds until death faces one of them and he says: «Now I repent;» nor of those who die while they are disbelievers. For them We have prepared a painful torment.»

An-Nisaa (Q4:17-18)

And the Prophet ﷺ said: "Allah accepts the repentance of the servant as long as he has not started gurgling."[168]

He also ﷺ said, "Certainly, Allah – the Mighty and Sublime – stretches His Hand in the night for the one who sinned in the day to turn in repentance, and stretches His Hand in the day that the one who sinned in the night may turn in repentance. And that (will continue) until the sun rises from its place of setting."[169]

168 *Al-Gargarah* (gurgling) is the hesitation of the soul in the throat. The Hadith is reported by Imam At-Tirmidhi in the Book on Supplications; Chapter on the Virtue of Repentance and Forgiveness, and What is Related about Allah's Mercy for His Servants: 5/ 547, and At-Tirmidhi said: A *Hasan Gareeb* Hadith.

169 Reported by Imam Muslim in his *Sahih*: The Book on Repentance: The Chapter on The Acceptance of Repentance from Sin even When it Reoccurs: 17/231.

8.3 Signs of True Repentance

True and sincere repentance has signs from which are:

1. **That the one Repenting Becomes Better than he was Before it.**

2. **That it is accompanied with the fear of retribution until he dies and hears the angels saying to him**

.... أَلَّا تَخَافُوا وَلَا تَحْزَنُوا وَأَبْشِرُوا بِالْجَنَّةِ الَّتِي كُنتُمْ تُوعَدُونَ ﴿٣٠﴾

«Fear not, nor grieve! But receive the glad tidings of Paradise which you have been promised!»

Fussilat (Q41:30)

Then should the fear go away.

3. **That he does More of Crying and Toning down before his Lord**

"And from the implications of true repentance – also –, is a special toning down that comes on the heart. Nothing is like it and no one feels it except the one who commits a sin (and repents sincerely). It is not attained by mere hunger or just love. It is rather something beyond all these. The heart feels completely deadened before the Lord and this could encapsulate all its aspects and hurl it before its Lord out of devotion and subservience.

There is nothing more beloved to Allah than this toning down, submission, reverence, humility, coming before Him, and resigning one's self to Him. How beautiful is it that the servant says words like these to Him in such circumstances, 'I beseech You by Your Might to show mercy to me. I ask You by Your Power and Wealth, for I am weak and in need of You. This is my lying and erring forelock before You. Your servants besides me are many but I have no Master except You. There is no shelter or refuge away from You except to You. I ask You as a poor, and I beseech You as a humble and lowly. I supplicate to You in the manner of the fearful and blind, in the manner of one on his knees, who fought against his will, shed tears for Your sake and humble his heart before You.'

These and others like it are the signs of accepted repentance; whoever has not noted that in his heart should query his repentance and rectify it. True repentance is actually so difficult to achieve but easy on the tongues and by claims. No truthful person cured anything more difficult for him to achieve as true and sincere repentance – *wa laa Haola walaa Quwwata illaa billaah*!"[170]

Umar bin Dhurr (d. 153) said, "Every sorrow wanes except the sorrow of the repenting servant from his sins."[171]

4. That the Vast Earth Should Become Straitened for the Sinner and He Should Feel Discomfort in His Heart until He Repents.

This is corroborated by Allah's saying regarding the three who did not join the Tabuk expedition رضي الله عنهم and Allah the Mighty and Sublime accepted their repentance:

170 *Tahdheeb Madaarij is-Saalikeen*: pg. 125, 126.
171 *Nuzhat ul-Fudalaa*: 2/548

...وَعَلَى ٱلثَّلَٰثَةِ ٱلَّذِينَ خُلِّفُوا۟ حَتَّىٰٓ إِذَا ضَاقَتْ عَلَيْهِمُ ٱلْأَرْضُ بِمَا رَحُبَتْ وَضَاقَتْ عَلَيْهِمْ أَنفُسُهُمْ وَظَنُّوٓا۟ أَن لَّا مَلْجَأَ مِنَ ٱللَّهِ إِلَّآ إِلَيْهِ ثُمَّ تَابَ عَلَيْهِمْ لِيَتُوبُوٓا۟ إِنَّ ٱللَّهَ هُوَ ٱلتَّوَّابُ ٱلرَّحِيمُ ﴿١١٨﴾

«And (He did forgive also) the three [who did not join the *Tabook* expedition (whom the Prophet s)] left (i.e. he did not give his judgement in their case, and their case was suspended for Allah's Decision) till for them the earth, vast as it is, was straitened and their ownselves were straitened to them, and they perceived that there is no fleeing from Allah, and no refuge but with Him. Then, He accepted their repentance that they might repent (unto Him). Verily, Allah is the One Who accepts repentance, Most Merciful.»

At-Tawbah (Q9:118)

5. Abandoning Sinful People

For whoever claims true repentance, and then keeps the company of the people who commit sin, or is regularly with them, such is one of two persons: One who is not truthful regarding his claims or one under the strong influence of desire which makes him go to the same set of people. Else, abandoning them is from the first and foremost things towards repentance.

Shaqeeq Al-Balkhee رحمه الله (d. 194 AH) said, "A sign of repentance is to weep regarding what happened, being afraid of falling into the sin, abandoning bad friends and keeping the company of the pious."[172]

172 *Nuzhat ul-Fudalaa*: 2/711.

8.4 Some Basic Rules and Words of Caution

1. **Whoever repents,** his sins are transformed to good deeds. Allah the Mighty and Sublime said:

إِلَّا مَن تَابَ وَءَامَنَ وَعَمِلَ عَمَلًا صَٰلِحًا فَأُوْلَٰٓئِكَ يُبَدِّلُ ٱللَّهُ سَيِّـَٔاتِهِمْ حَسَنَٰتٍ ۗ
وَكَانَ ٱللَّهُ غَفُورًا رَّحِيمًا ﴿٧٠﴾

«Except those who repent and believe (in Islamic Monotheism), and do righteous deeds, for those, Allah will change their sins into good deeds, and Allah is Oft-Forgiving, Most Merciful.»

Al-Furqan (Q25:70)

2. **The greatest** form of repentance is *Nasuh* (sincere) repentance; and it has been described as the repentance from sin without returning to it as the milk does not return to the udder. Ibn al-Qayyim stated that sincere repentance is by three things: that it entails all sins; that is, it does not leave out any sin. One should truly resolve to abandon it without ever returning to it and purify it from every defect and taint.

   Contrary to the one who repents to preserve his rank and honour or status and office or to preserve his powers and wealth or to make the people praise him or to avoid their abuse. Or not to be overpowered by the vulgar or for his incapability and inability and things like that of the defects that impact its being truly for Allah – the Mighty and Sublime.

This is the most perfect form of repentance.[173]

3. **The prohibited** things from which the servant needs to repent from and around which the details of the Major sins are centered are twelve in kind and are all mentioned in Allah's Book. They are:

    - *Kufr* (Disbelief),
    - *Shirk* (Associating partners with Allah),
    - *Nifaaq* (Hypocrisy),
    - *Fusuq* (Wantonness),
    - *'Isyaan* (Rebellion),
    - *Ithm* (Iniquity),
    - *'Udwaan* (Aggression),
    - *Fahshaa* (Illicit Intercourse),
    - *Munkar* (Distasteful Deed),
    - *Bag'y* (Oppression),
    - *Qaol 'alaa Allahi bilaa 'Ilm* (Saying about Allah without knowledge) and
    - *'Ittibaa'u gayra Sabeel il-Mu'mineen* (following other than the way of the believers).[174]

---

173 *Tahdheeb Madaarij is-Saalikeen*: pg. 178, 179.
174 The previous reference: 191

4. **The most beneficial** and perfect for the servant is that he should repent from Major and Minor sins all together sincerely. However, a person may repent only from Major sins and not the Minor sins. He could also repent from one or more Major sins while he still commits other Major sins, not having repented from them. Similarly, he could repent from Minor sins and not from the Major sins. Each of these happen to the servant – Allah alone is the Source of Help and unto Him is reliance.

5. **There are those** who are unable to repent despite affirming its significance and great excellence owing to the over-bearing influence of his desire. For such, he should follow sin with good deeds and be from those who:

.... خَلَطُوا۟ عَمَلًا صَٰلِحًا وَءَاخَرَ سَيِّئًا عَسَى ٱللَّهُ أَن يَتُوبَ عَلَيْهِمْ ۚ إِنَّ ٱللَّهَ
غَفُورٌ رَّحِيمٌ ﴿١٠٢﴾

«They have mixed a deed that was righteous with another that was evil. Perhaps Allah will turn unto them in forgiveness. Surely, Allah is Oft-Forgiving, Most Merciful».[175]

At-Tawbah (Q9:102)

Perhaps Allah will make the path of repentance easy for him by his continuously following up sins with good deeds and if he does not repent until he dies, perhaps, his good deeds will outweigh the sins on the Scale and he thereby succeeds by Allah's favour and mercy. Otherwise, he is in great danger!

175 See: *Ithaaf us-Saadat il-Muttaqeen*: 1/749.

6. **The repenting** servant has to leave bad company and that is for two reasons:

   The First: because they will make him remember sin, prompt him to it and motivate him regarding it.

   The Second: because leaving them is evidence for the trueness of his repentance and his turning towards his Lord. Else, how will he claim repentance while following the path of sin and its people? We had discussed abandoning sinful people.

7. **The author of Al-Qaamus said:** *Tawbah* (Repentance) is mentioned in the Qur'aan in three forms:

   The First: To mean pardon and forgiveness; and this is followed with the particle, *'alaa*:

... فَتَابَ عَلَيْكُمْ ... ﴿٥٥﴾

«Then He accepted your repentance...»

Al-Baqarah (Q2:54)

And:

... أَوْ يَتُوبَ عَلَيْهِمْ ... ﴿١٢٨﴾

«He turns in mercy to (pardons) them...»

Aal Imran (Q3:128)

And:

.... وَيَتُوبُ ٱللَّهُ عَلَىٰ مَن يَشَآءُۗ .... ﴿١٥﴾

«Allah accepts the repentance of whom He wills...»

At-Tawbah (Q9:15)

The Second: To mean; to turn towards; and that is followed with the particle *ilaa*;

.... تُبْتُ إِلَيْكَ .... ﴿١٤٣﴾

«I turn to You in repentance.»

Al-A'raf (Q7:143)

.... فَتُوبُوٓاْ إِلَىٰ بَارِئِكُمْ .... ﴿٥٤﴾

«So turn in repentance to your Creator.»

Al-Baqarah (Q2:54)

.... وَتُوبُوٓاْ إِلَى ٱللَّهِ .... ﴿٣١﴾

«And all of you beg Allah to forgive you.»

An-Nur (Q24:31)

The Third: to mean regretting over failure; and this is neither followed with *ilaa* nor *'alaa*:

إِلَّا ٱلَّذِينَ تَابُواْ وَأَصْلَحُواْ ... ﴿١٦٠﴾

«Except those who repent and do righteous deeds…»

Al-Baqarah (Q2:160)

.... فَإِن تُبْتُمْ فَهُوَ خَيْرٌ لَّكُمْ .... ﴿٣﴾

«…so if you repent, it is better for you…»

At-Tawbah (Q9:3)

8. **Allah (the Exalted)** forgives every sincerely repenting servant such that he becomes free from punishment for the sin if he repents before the Authority gets aware and before he is brought before it. Except the following kinds of people:

   i. The Magicians, and that is because, magic is disbelief in addition to the fact that it is not possible to be sure of the repentance of the magician and his abandoning the evil.

   ii. Whoever abuses a prophet and was basically a Muslim; for he will be killed.

   iii. A *Zindeeq*; and that is the person who does not consider any religion rightful or one who does not actually have a religion and in that, claims Islam.

iv. A *Raafidee* who abuses the companions; and that is in the view of Abu Hanifa ﷺ.[176]

The repentance of these people is not accepted in this world; rather, they are to be killed. As for that between them and Allah (the Exalted), it is a different matter, for Allah Sees and is Aware of what is in their hearts of true or false repentance and will treat them on the Day of Resurrection based on what was established in their hearts before they were killed.

Some Stories of Repentant Servants

1. **Abu Sa'eed Al-Khudree** ﷺ reported that the Prophet ﷺ said, "There was a man among the people before you who killed ninety-nine persons and enquired about the most learned person on earth. He was directed to a monk. He went to him and said that he killed ninety-nine persons. Does he have a chance to repent? He said, 'No', and so, he killed him and made him the hundredth person. Then, he enquired about the most learned person on earth and he was directed to a learned man. He said that he had killed hundred persons; does he have a chance of repentance? He said, 'Yes, no one should prevent you from repenting. Go to such-and-such a land. In it, there are people who worship Allah, worship with them and do not return to your land for it is an evil place.'

   So, he proceeded and after he travelled half the distance, the angel of death came to him (and took his life). Then the angels of mercy and the angels of punishment contented regarding him. The angels of mercy said, 'He

176 *Ahkaam ut-Tawbah* by Shaykh AbdulGaniyy An-Naabulsee: pg 94 – 98 with modification.

came repentant, turning sincerely towards Allah (the Exalted).' The angels of punishment said, 'He had never done any good deed.' Then an angel in human form came and they made him the arbiter and he said, 'Measure the distance between the two lands; to whichever of them both he is closer, that is where he belongs to.' So, they measured it and found that he was closer to the land which he intended and the angels of mercy took charge of him."

In another version, it says, "He was closer to the land of the righteous by the hand span and thus, was counted amongst its people."

In another version, "Allah inspired this (part of the land) to expand and that, to shrink, and then said, 'Measure between them' and they found him closer by the hand span, and he was forgiven."

Still in another report, Al-Hasan said, "It was mentioned to us that when the angel of death approached him, he crawled with his chest."[177]

2. **Buraydah** ﷺ said, "Maa'iz bin Maalik came to the Prophet ﷺ and said, 'Please purify me.' He said, 'Woe be to you,[178] go back and seek forgiveness from Allah, and repent unto him.' Shortly after, he came back and said, 'O Messenger of Allah, purify me.' The Prophet ﷺ retorted, 'Woe be to you, go back and seek forgiveness from Allah, and repent unto Him.'"

177 *At-Targeeb wat-Tarheeb*: 4/101, 102; and Haafidh Al-Mundhiree said: Reported by Al-Bukhaari, Muslim and Ibn Maajah similarly.

178 The actual Arabic expression, *Waylak* or *Wayhak* are not used to imply their lexical meaning. They are rather used to express caution to a person groundlessly falling into error. (TN)

He said, "He soon returned and said again, 'O Messenger of Allah, purify me.' Then the Prophet ﷺ said the like of what he had said until, at the fourth time, Allah's Messenger ﷺ asked him, 'Of what should I purify you?' He answered, 'From fornication.' Then the Messenger of Allah ﷺ asked, 'Is he mad?' and he was told that he is not. He enquired, 'Did he drink alcohol?' A man stood up and smelt him but did not perceive any odor of alcohol.

So, Allah's Messenger ﷺ said, 'Did you commit illicit sexual intercourse?' He said: 'Yes.' He then ordered that he should be stoned to death. The people were divided into two groups regarding his affair: some said, 'He is destroyed, consumed by his sin.' Others said, 'What a beautiful manner of repentance by Maa'iz, he came to the prophet and placed his hand in his and then said, *stone me to death*!'"

Buraydah went on, "So, they continued like that for two or three days. Thereafter, Allah's Messenger ﷺ came while they were sitting, said the *salam* to them, sat down and said, 'Seek (Allah's) forgiveness for Maa'iz bin Maalik.'" He said: "And they all said, 'May Allah forgive Maa'iz bin Maalik.' He said: "And Allah's Messenger ﷺ said, 'He has repented in a manner that, were it distributed among a nation, it will suffice them.'"[179]

3. **Buraydah** رضي الله عنه who said: "The woman from the Gaamid tribe came and said, 'O Messenger of Allah, I have committed illicit sexual intercourse, please purify me.' He turned her back. On the following day, she (came again)

179 Reported by Imam Muslim in his *Sahih*: The Book on Legal Punishments: The Chapter on the One who confesses Committing Illicit Sexual Intercourse: 11/345.

and said, 'Why did you turn me back, O Messenger of Allah? Perhaps you want to turn me back as you turned back Maa'iz, for by Allah, I am pregnant (from the intercourse).'"

He ﷺ said, "Well, if you do not accept (my counsel), then, go and come back after you have given birth." When she delivered, she came along with the child, wrapped in a piece of cloth and said, 'I have delivered.' He said, "Go and suckle it until you wean it." After the weaning, she came to him with the child with a piece of bread and said, 'I have weaned it, O Messenger of Allah, it (the child) has started taking food.' So, he entrusted the child to one of the Muslims, commanded that a hole be dug to the level of her chest and ordered the people to stone her. Khaalid bin Waleed got a boulder and stoned her head. The blood splashed on his head and he abused her. The Prophet ﷺ then heard his abusing her and said, "Take it easy, O Khaalid, for I swear by the One in whose hand is my soul, she has repented in a manner that if the tax collector repented similarly, he would be forgiven."

In another version, it said: "Then he observed the funeral prayer for her. 'Umar observed, 'You are performing the funeral prayer for her, O Prophet of Allah, when she had committed illicit sexual intercourse?' He ﷺ remarked, 'She has repented in a manner that, were it distributed among seventy persons from the people of Madeenah, it will suffice them. Have you found any repentance better than her giving herself up for the sake of Allah (the Exalted)?'"[180]

180 Reported by Imam Muslim in his *Sahih*: the Book on Legal punishments: The Chapter on the one who Confesses Committing Illicit Sexual Intercourse: 11/347.

4. **The repentance** of Ka'b bin Maalik ﵁. His story is tremendously beneficial. I will quote it completely for what it contains of lessons and admonitions. Ka'b bin Maalik said, "I never stayed behind Allah's Messenger ﷺ in any military expedition he made but in Tabuk. Except that I stayed behind in Badr and nobody was blamed for being absent from it. Allah's Messenger ﷺ and the Muslims had set out intending the caravan of Quraysh until Allah made them face their enemy unexpectedly.

   I was present with Allah's Messenger ﷺ on the Night of 'Aqaba when we took the convenant for Islam, and it was dearer to me than participating in the Battle of Badr, although Badr was more famous among the people than it (the Night of 'Aqaba).

   My situation when I tarried behind the Messenger of Allah ﷺ in expedition of Tabuk was that I had never been wealthier or stronger than when I stayed behind him in that campaign. By Allah, I had never possessed two riding camels simultaneously until I had them in that expedition.

   Allah's Messenger ﷺ went for the campaign in intense hot weather. The journey was long and the land was wild and he had to face a large army. So, he made the matter known to the Muslims so that they could make adequate preparations for the campaign. He told them the direction in which he resolved to go. The Muslims who accompanied Allah's Messenger were plenty such that a record book - he meant a register – will not contain their list."

   Ka'b said, "Hardly a man wanted to be absent than he thought that his absence would be hidden to him unless revelation came from Allah the Mighty and Sublime about it.

Allah's Messenger ﷺ set out on that expedition when the fruits were ripe and shadows were pleasant, and I was inclined to them. The Messenger of Allah ﷺ made arrangements and the Muslims with him. I started in the morning to prepare with them and I would return not having done anything. I would say to myself: I am able to do that if I determine. I continued doing this (delaying) while people were still preparing.

Then Allah's Messenger ﷺ set out on a morning along with the Muslims, but I had not made any preparations. I went early in the morning and came back without decision.

I went on doing so until they hastened and went far in the campaign. I also resolved to depart to catch up with them, but I wished I had done so. Yet, I was unable to do so. Whenever I went out among people, after the departure of Allah's Messenger ﷺ , I became gloomy that I didn't find any one similar to me except a man despised for his hypocrisy or a person amongst the weak who was excused by Allah.

The Messenger of Allah ﷺ didn't take notice of me until he had arrived Tabuk. While he was sitting among the people in Tabuk, he said, 'What has Ka'b bin Maalik done?' A man from Banu Salama said: 'O Messenger of Allah, the wonder of his garments and looking at his sides have hindered him.' Mu'adh bin Jabal رضي الله عنه then said to him: 'What a bad thing you told! By Allah, O Messenger of Allah, we knew nothing about him but good.' Allah's Messenger ﷺ kept silent.

While he was in this situation he saw a person dressed in white appearing with the phantom, and the Messenger of Allah ﷺ said, 'May it be Abu Khaythama', and it was Abu Khaythama Al-Ansaree, who gave a measure of dates in charity and the hypocrites defamed him.

Ka'b bin Maalik said, "When the news got to me that Allah's Messenger ﷺ was on his way back from Tabuk, I became anguished. I started recollecting false stories and would say, 'How could I save myself from his discontent the next day?' For that, I resorted to men of counsel of my relatives. But when I was told that Allah's Messenger ﷺ was about to come, untrue thought vanished from my mind, and I became sure that I would never be saved from him (his anger) within a thing including lying, so I made up my mind to tell him the truth.

In the morning, the Messenger of Allah ﷺ arrived. He used, after returning from a travel, to go to the mosque first; he would pray two units of prayer then sit to listen to people's issues. After he did that, the people who stayed behind him started to come to him excusing and swearing. They were more than eighty-some persons. So, Allah's Messenger ﷺ accepted their excuses, accepted their allegiance and sought forgiveness for them, and left their secrets to Allah, until I came. When I greeted, he smiled a wrathful smile and then said: 'Come on.' I advanced walking until I sat in front of him. He asked me: 'Why did keep you back? Hadn't you bought what to ride?'"

Ka'b continued, "I said, "O Messenger of Allah, by Allah, had I sat in the presence of any one in the world other than you, I would have been able to avoid his anger with an excuse, and I had ability to argue, but, by Allah,

I believe if I bring an untrue account, so that you be pleased with me, Allah will soon make you dislike me. But if I tell the true tale you may be angry with me, but I beg that Allah makes its consequences well. By Allah, I had no excuse. By Allah, I had never been stronger or wealthier than when I stayed behind you.

Allah's Messenger ﷺ said, 'This one told the truth; so depart until Allah judges in your case.' I started out and some men of Banee Salama followed me hastily and said, 'By Allah, we didn't ever know you to have committed a sin before this: you were unable to bring an excuse to Allah's Messenger ﷺ as those who stayed behind him had done. It would have been sufficient to abolish your sin that Allah's Messenger ﷺ would have sought forgiveness for you.'"

He said, "By Allah, they went on reproving me until I thought of returning to Allah's Messenger ﷺ and disclaiming myself. Then, I asked them, 'Has anyone else faced the same case with me?' They said, 'Yes, two persons; they said what you said and the like of what was said to you was said to them.' I said: Who are they? They said, 'Murara bin Ar-Rabi' Al-'Aamiree and Hilaal bin Umayya Al-Waaqifee.'" He said, "So, they mentioned these two pious persons who took part in the battle of Badr, and there was an example for me in them." He said, "I departed when they named them to me.

Allah's Messenger ﷺ prohibited the Muslims to speak to us; we the three, from amongst those who had remained behind him." He went on, "So, the People avoided us. Their attitude towards us changed until the world seemed to treat me with contempt, it didn't look like the one that I knew. We spent fifty nights in this situation.

As for my two companions (i.e. who also stayed back and gave no excuses), they yielded and confined themselves within their houses weeping (most of the time). But in my case, I was the younger and more tolerant. So, I would go out to perform the prayer, move around the market places and no one would utter a word to me. Also I would come to Allah's Messenger ﷺ give the *salaams* to him during his gathering after the prayer, and wonder within myself: Did he move his lips retorting my greeting or not? Then, I prayed near him and looked at him stealthily. When I was engaged in my prayer he looked at me and when I turned my face towards him he turned his eyes away from me.

When this estrangement of the Muslims lasted long towards me, I walked until I scaled upon the wall of Abee Qataadah's house, who was my cousin and the dearest of all to me. I greeted him, and by Allah, he didn't reply my greeting. Then I said to him: Aba Qataadah, I adjure you by Allah, don't you know certainly that I love Allah and his Messenger?" He said, "He kept silent. I adjured him again and he remained silent and then, I adjured him and he said, 'Allah and his Messenger know best.' Tears rolled down from my eyes and I turned back climbing down the wall.

While I was walking in the bazaar of Madeenah, there was a Nabataean from among the Nabataeans of Shaam, who had come to sell foodstuff in Madeenah, inquiring, 'Who could lead me to Ka'b bin Maalik?' People began directing him until he reached me and handed me a letter from the King of Ghassan. Being knowledgeable, I read it and it contained, 'After that, it has been conveyed to us that your companion (Allah's Messenger) had treated you coolly, while Allah has not created you in a place of humiliation or forfeiture. So come to us and we give comfort to you.' I said when I read it, 'this is also an adversity'; so I went with it to the kiln where I burnt it.

When forty days out of the fifty had passed away and revelation took long time with no descent, then the envoy of Allah's Messenger ﷺ came to me, and he said, 'Allah's Messenger ﷺ commands you to dissociate from your wife.' I asked, 'Should I divorce her or what should I do?' He said, 'No, but only remain separate from her without copulation.' He sent a similar message to both of my companions." Ka'b said, "So, I said to my wife, 'Go to your parents and stay there with them until Allah judges in this case.'

The wife of Hilaal bin Umayya came to Allah's Messenger ﷺ and said, 'O Messenger of Allah, Hilaal bin Umayya is a wasted aged man with no servant. Do you dislike that I serve him?' He said, 'No, but He shouldn't come near to you.' She said, 'By Allah, he hasn't any instinct, and by Allah, he continued weeping since that thing took place till now.'

Some of my relatives said to me, 'If only you asked permission from Allah's Messenger ﷺ with regard to your wife for he has permitted the wife of Hilaal bin Umayya to serve him.' I said, 'I wouldn't ask permission from Allah's Messenger ﷺ concerning her, for I can't tell what Allah's Messenger may say if I seek permission since I am a young man. I spent ten nights in this case and thus fifty nights had passed since when we weren't allowed to be spoken to.

Ka'b bin Malik went on, "In the early morning of the fiftieth night I prayed the dawn prayer on the roof of one of our houses. While I was sitting in the condition, which was described by Allah, the Mighty and Sublime, about us that I myself was straitened and the earth seems to be limited despite its vastness. I heard the voice of a yeller who came over Sal'[181] crying as high as he could, 'O Ka'b bin Maalik, be delighted!' Then I fell on the ground in prostration, and recognized that relief had come."

He said, "Allah's Messenger ﷺ announced the acceptance of our repentance by Allah, as he prayed the dawn prayer, so people set out breaking the good news to us. Harbingers of good news went towards my two companions and a person galloped a horse towards me. A courier from the Aslam tribe also came towards mean and climbed over the mountain; the voice was quicker than the horse. When the person whose voice I heard giving the news of joy to me came to me, I removed my two cloths and dressed him with them for this good news. And by Allah, I possessed no other than the two on that day.

I borrowed two clothes, put them on and hurried to Allah's Messenger ﷺ. On my way, I met groups of people congratulating me on the repentance, saying: 'Felicitate for the acceptance of your repentance by Allah.' Until I entered the mosque, there Allah's Messenger ﷺ was sitting surrounded by people. Talha bin 'Ubaydullah (may be pleased with him) rushed towards me, shook hands with me, and congratulated me. By Allah, no one out of the emigrants stood up except him."

181 A known mountain in Madeenah

Ka'b never forgot it (i.e. the hearty reception) from Talha.

Ka'b said, "When I greeted Allah's Messenger ﷺ and his face was glistening because of pleasure, he said, 'Be delighted with the best of all days that you passed since your mother gave birth to you.'" He said, "I asked, 'Is it from you, O Messenger of Allah or from Allah?' He said, 'No, it is from Allah.' And when Allah's Messenger ﷺ was happy his face became brightened as if it was a piece of a moon, and we knew that." Ka'b carried on, "When I sat before him I said, 'O Allah's Messenger: It is a part of my repentance to give all my wealth in charity (for the sake of) Allah and His Messenger ﷺ. So, Allah's Messenger ﷺ said, 'Keep some of your property with you, for it is beneficial for you.'" Ka'b said, "So, I answered, I will keep my allotment in Khaybar.

I said, 'O Messenger of Allah, certainly, Allah has salvaged me for being truthful, and so, from my repentance is not to tell anything but truth as long as I live." He said, "By Allah, I donot know if any one of the Muslims was put to test in regard to telling the truth more than I was, since I told that Allah's Messenger ﷺ till this day. By Allah, since I mentioned this to Allah's Messenger ﷺ up till this day, I have never told a lie, and I beg Allah – the Mighty and Sublime, to preserve me for the rest of my life."

Ka'b bin Maalik said, "Allah – the Mighty and Sublime - revealed:

لَّقَد تَّابَ ٱللَّهُ عَلَى ٱلنَّبِيِّ وَٱلۡمُهَٰجِرِينَ وَٱلۡأَنصَارِ ٱلَّذِينَ ٱتَّبَعُوهُ فِي سَاعَةِ ٱلۡعُسۡرَةِ

لَّقَد تَّابَ ٱللَّهُ عَلَى ٱلنَّبِيِّ وَٱلْمُهَٰجِرِينَ وَٱلْأَنصَارِ ٱلَّذِينَ ٱتَّبَعُوهُ فِي سَاعَةِ ٱلْعُسْرَةِ
مِنۢ بَعْدِ مَا كَادَ يَزِيغُ قُلُوبُ فَرِيقٍ مِّنْهُمْ ثُمَّ تَابَ عَلَيْهِمْ إِنَّهُۥ بِهِمْ رَءُوفٌ
رَّحِيمٌ ﴿١١٧﴾ وَعَلَى ٱلثَّلَٰثَةِ ٱلَّذِينَ خُلِّفُوا۟ حَتَّىٰٓ إِذَا ضَاقَتْ عَلَيْهِمُ ٱلْأَرْضُ بِمَا
رَحُبَتْ وَضَاقَتْ عَلَيْهِمْ أَنفُسُهُمْ وَظَنُّوٓا۟ أَن لَّا مَلْجَأَ مِنَ ٱللَّهِ إِلَّآ إِلَيْهِ ثُمَّ تَابَ
عَلَيْهِمْ .... ﴿١١٨﴾

«Allah has forgiven the Prophet ﷺ, the *Muhaajirun* (Muslim emigrants who left their homes and came to Al-Madeenah) and the *Ansaar* (Muslims of Al-Madeenah) who followed him (Muhammad ﷺ) in the time of distress (Tabuk expedition, etc.), after the hearts of a party of them had nearly deviated (from the Right Path), but He accepted their repentance. Certainly, He is unto them full of Kindness, Most Merciful. And (He did forgive also) the three [who did not join the Tabuk expedition (whom the Prophet ﷺ)] left (i.e. he did not give his judgment in their case, and their case was suspended for Allah's Decision) till for them the earth, vast as it is, was straitened and their ownselves were straitened to them…»

Until it reached:

يَٰٓأَيُّهَا ٱلَّذِينَ ءَامَنُوا۟ ٱتَّقُوا۟ ٱللَّهَ وَكُونُوا۟ مَعَ ٱلصَّٰدِقِينَ ﴿١١٩﴾

«O you who believe! Be afraid of Allah, and be with those who are true (in words and deeds).»

At-Tawbah (Q9:117-119)

Ka'b said, "By Allah, since Allah guided me to Islam, Allah has not granted me a favour, greater in myself than telling the truth to Allah's Messenger ﷺ and not bringing a false narration that I will be ruined as had happened to those who told lies. Allah addressed those who told lies when He sent revelation with the harshest that He addressed to a person. Allah – Glorious is He - said:

سَيَحْلِفُونَ بِٱللَّهِ لَكُمْ إِذَا ٱنقَلَبْتُمْ إِلَيْهِمْ لِتُعْرِضُوا۟ عَنْهُمْ ۖ فَأَعْرِضُوا۟ عَنْهُمْ ۖ إِنَّهُمْ
رِجْسٌ ۖ وَمَأْوَىٰهُمْ جَهَنَّمُ جَزَآءًۢ بِمَا كَانُوا۟ يَكْسِبُونَ ﴿٩٥﴾ يَحْلِفُونَ لَكُمْ لِتَرْضَوْا۟
عَنْهُمْ ۖ فَإِن تَرْضَوْا۟ عَنْهُمْ فَإِنَّ ٱللَّهَ لَا يَرْضَىٰ عَنِ ٱلْقَوْمِ ٱلْفَـٰسِقِينَ ﴿٩٦﴾

«They will swear by Allah to you (Muslims) when you return to them, that you may turn away from them. So turn away from them. Surely, they are *Rijsun* (impure) because of their evil deeds], and Hell is their dwelling place, - a recompense for that which they used to earn. They (the hypocrites) swear to you (Muslims) that you may be pleased with them, but if you are pleased with them, certainly Allah is not pleased with the people who are *Al-Faasiqun* (rebellious, disobedient to Allah).»

At-Tawbah (Q9:95-96)

Ka'b said, "We, the three, were postponed apart from the matter of those who swore to the Messenger of Allah ﷺ, so the Messenger of Allah ﷺ accepted their pardons, pledged allegiance for them, and asked forgiveness for them. Allah's Messenger ﷺ delayed our case till Allah judged regarding it, and concerning this, Allah – the Mighty and Sublime – said:

.... وَعَلَى ٱلثَّلَٰثَةِ ٱلَّذِينَ خُلِّفُوا۟ .... ﴿١١٨﴾

«And (He did forgive also) the three who stayed behind... «

At-Tawbah (Q9:118)

The reference here is not to our staying back from the campaign but to his postponing of our matter after that of those who swore and brought excuses that he accepted."[182]

5. **The repentance** of Zaadhaan Al-Kindee, one of the eminent scholars among the *Taabi'een*. He died in the year 290 AH – may Allah shower blessings on him. He repented in the hands of Ibn Mas'ud رضي الله عنه. Zaadhaan said, "I was a young boy with a nice voice and great ability to play the lute. Once, I was with one of my friends, we had wine while I entertained them with music. Then, Ibn Mas'ud passed by us and hit the wine container wasting its content and broke the lute. He then then said, 'If what is heard of your nice voice, O young boy, is of the Qur'aan, I wish I was like you.' He then moved on. So, I asked my companions, 'Who is this?' They said, 'This is Ibn Mas'ud.'

   So, it occurred to me that I turn to Allah in repentance. I followed him crying and held his cloth. He turned

182 Reported by Imam Muslim in his *Sahih*: The Book on Repentance: The Chapter on the Repentance of Ka'b bin Maalik and his two Companions: 17/239 – 247.

towards me, embraced me and wept and then said, 'The one loved by Allah is welcomed, sit (here).' Then he entered and brought me some dates."[183]

6. **The repentance** of Fudayl bin 'Iyyaad (d. 186): He had been a high-way robber "and the cause of his repentance was that, he was interested in a girl and while he climbed the fence to get to her, he heard a reciter reading:

أَلَمْ يَأْنِ لِلَّذِينَ ءَامَنُوٓا۟ أَن تَخْشَعَ قُلُوبُهُمْ لِذِكْرِ ٱللَّهِ .... ﴿١٦﴾

«Has not the time come for the hearts of those who believe (in the Oneness of Allah - Islamic Monotheism) to be affected by Allah's Reminder (this Qur'aan)...»

Al-Hadid (Q57:16)

When he heard it, he said, 'Yes, O my Lord, the time has come.' So, he returned and the night came upon him in a dilapidated building where he found some travellers. One of them said, 'Let's proceed' and others said, 'Let's wait till dawn for Fudayl is on the way, he will rob us.' Fudayl said, "So, I pondered and said (to myself), 'I move around perpetrating evil in the night and here are some of the Muslims who are afraid of me and I do not think that Allah brought me to them except to make me repent. O Allah, I turn towards you in repentance and from my repentance is to take neighbourhood in the Sanctified House.'"[184]

183 *Nuzhat ul-Fudalaa*: 1/386.
184 *Nuzhat ul-Fudalaa*: 2/ 660

Chapter 9

At-Tawakkul (Reliance on Allah)

It is a great heart-related worship which is misunderstood by some group of worshippers and ascetics and some among the common people. They generally hold two opposite positions on this issue: one of excessiveness, and the other of laxity missing the middle-course which is the attribute of this blessed *Ummah*.

"The need for the Muslim who is upon the path of Allah for reliance on Allah is great, especially in the aspects of sustenance which has occupied the intellects and minds of the people. Many of them – rather, most of them – got therefrom, weakness of the body, grief, sleeplessness in the night and toil in the day. In some cases, some of them accept disgracing themselves, bending their heads and giving their honour for bread and butter which they think lies in the hand of a creature like themselves which he would only if he wills and deny them if he wills. So, their life and that of their children are in such hands.

Even, sometimes, one of them may go ahead and give himself the verdict to consume ill-gotten wealth, take bribe, legitimize interest and take wealth from people in prohibited manners for the fear of what happens to him when he grows old after his youthful age, or if he falls sick after good health or becomes jobless after having worked or because he fears for his weak offspring after him. Nevertheless, the way out of all these actually, is totally placing reliance in Allah – the most High."[185]

Ibn al-Qayyim explained:

> "Reliance on Allah (*At-Tawakkul*) is a half of the *Deen*, and the other half is turning towards Allah (*Al-Inaabah*). So, the *Deen* is seeking for assistance (*Al-Isti'aanah*) and worship (*Al-'Ibaadah*).[186] The *Tawakkul* is the *Isti'aanah* and the *Inaabah* is the *'Ibaadah*. In fact, it (i.e. the reliance on Allah, *At-Tawakkul*) is pure servitude and affirmation of Allah's oneness if a person truly upholds it."[187]

9.1 The Meaning of *At-Tawakkul*

Lexically, "It is said, *Tawakkala bi al-Amr* when he guarantees doing it, and *Wakkaltu Amree ilaa Fulaan* i.e. I entrusted my affair to so-and-so and rely on him regarding it and *Wakala Fulaanun Fulaanan* when he leaves his matter to him trusting in his (i.e. the other's) ability or out of his inability to dispose the affair himself."

Technically, "the one who relies on Allah: is the one who recognizes that Allah takes care of his sustenance and (other) affairs and so, depends on Him alone and never depends on other than Him." "*At-Tawakkul* is essentially the true dependence of the heart on Allah – the Mighty

185 *At-Tawakkul* by Dr. Yusuf Al-Qaradawi, pg. 9-10

186 Ibn ul-Qayyim took that from His saying about the believers: **"You (Alone) we worship, and You (Alone) we ask for help (for each and everything)."**

187 *Tahdheeb Madaarij is-Saalikeen*: pg. 336.

and Sublime – regarding getting benefits and putting away harm in all of the matters of this world and the hereafter. Depending on Him regarding all affairs and truly believing that no one truly gives, denies, harms or benefits except Him."[188]

It is said that, "It is the Heart's recognition of the Lord's sufficiency for the servant."[189] *At-Tawakkul* is "a person's surrendering his affair and not contending with his Controller, depending on Him in it and leaving one's affairs away from being merely out of his own ability and power to it's being disposed by his Lord, that He and not him is in-charge. This is what *At-Tawakkul* means."[190]

9.2 Levels of People Having *At-Tawakkul*

1. **The pious servants**

   Those who "rely on Him about *Eeman*, assistance of His religion, uplifting His word, fighting His enemies, and regarding His favours and the implementation of His orders.

2. **Below them is the one who rely on Him about his steadfastness** and keeping his condition with Allah away from the people.

3. **And below them are those who rely on Him about a particular thing they need from Him of wealth or health** or help over enemy or spouse or offspring or

188 I have quoted these definitions of *At-Tawakkul* from the introductory notes of *Ustadh* Jaasim Al-Fuhayd to the book: *At-Tawakkul 'alaa Allah* by Haafidh Ibn Abee Dunyaa: pg. 31.

189 *Tahdheeb Madaarij is-Saalikeen*: pg. 336.

190 The previous reference.

things like that.

The best form of *At-Tawakkul* is that regarding the obligations – I mean – obligations of Allah, the obligations of the creatures and those of the self.

The most beneficial of it is: relying on Allah about outward impacts of religious benefits or putting away harm from the aspects of the religion. It is the Prophets' way of reliance on Allah regarding the establishment of His religion and preventing the evil by its people on the earth. This form of reliance on Allah is from the legacies of the Prophets – peace and blessings be upon them.

Then, people are of different levels of reliance on Allah based on their intentions and purposes."[191]

There are many narrations in the Qur'aan about *At-Tawakkul*: the lives of the Messengers with their people; those who aided them and those who were their enemies illustrate *At-Tawakkul*. The efforts of the pious mentioned in the Qur'aan, like the one who believed amongst the people of Pharaoh, the believer among the *Ashaab al-Qaryah* (the People of the City) in *Surah Ya-Seen* and others demonstrate *At-Tawakkul*.

Many verses of the Noble Qur'aan encourage relying on Allah, its virtues and perfection. Allah (the Exalted) said,

.... وَعَلَى ٱللَّهِ فَتَوَكَّلُوٓاْ إِن كُنتُم مُّؤْمِنِينَ ﴿٢٣﴾

191 *Tahdheeb Madaarij is-Saalikeen*: pg. 334

«...And put your trust in Allah if you are believers indeed.»

Al-Ma'idah (Q5:23)

He the Mighty and Sublime also said,

وَيَرْزُقْهُ مِنْ حَيْثُ لَا يَحْتَسِبُ ۚ وَمَن يَتَوَكَّلْ عَلَى ٱللَّهِ فَهُوَ حَسْبُهُۥٓ .... ﴿٣﴾

«And whosoever puts his trust in Allah, then He will suffice him...»

At-Talaq (Q65:3)

He while explaining the supplication of His friends, said:

.... رَّبَّنَا عَلَيْكَ تَوَكَّلْنَا وَإِلَيْكَ أَنَبْنَا وَإِلَيْكَ ٱلْمَصِيرُ ﴿٤﴾

«Our Lord! In You (Alone) we put our trust, and to You (Alone) we turn in repentance, and to You (Alone) is (our) final Return.»

Al-Mumtahanah (Q60:4)

He – Glorious is He – said to His Messenger ﷺ, said,

.... فَإِذَا عَزَمْتَ فَتَوَكَّلْ عَلَى ٱللَّهِ ۚ إِنَّ ٱللَّهَ يُحِبُّ ٱلْمُتَوَكِّلِينَ ﴿١٥٩﴾

«Then when you have taken a decision, put your trust in Allah, certainly, Allah loves those who put their trust (in Him).»

Aal Imran (Q3:159)

Allah – Glorious is He – while praising the companions, said,

ٱلَّذِينَ قَالَ لَهُمُ ٱلنَّاسُ إِنَّ ٱلنَّاسَ قَدْ جَمَعُواْ لَكُمْ فَٱخْشَوْهُمْ فَزَادَهُمْ إِيمَـٰنًا
وَقَالُواْ حَسْبُنَا ٱللَّهُ وَنِعْمَ ٱلْوَكِيلُ ﴿١٧٣﴾

«Those (i.e. believers) unto whom the people (hypocrites) said, 'Verily, the people (pagans) have gathered against you (a great army), therefore, fear them. But it (only) increased them in Faith, and they said: 'Allah (Alone) is Sufficient for us, and He is the Best Disposer of affairs (for us).'»

Aal Imran (Q3:173)

And very many other verses.

The Prophet ﷺ explained *At-Tawakkul* and extolled it. And why not, while one of his names is *Al-Mutawakkil* (The reliant on Allah) as is reported in some narrations.

Similarly, he ﷺ used to supplicate to Allah – (the Exalted) – demonstrating his reliance on his Beloved to the *Ummah*, saying: "*Allahumma laka Aslamtu, wa bika Aamantu, wa 'alayka Tawakaltu, wa ilayka Anabtu wa laka Khaasamtu* (meaning: O Allah, unto You I submit, in You I believe, and on You I rely, to You I turn towards and to You I lay my complains)."[192]

He ﷺ would order his companions to rely on Allah (the Exalted), saying, "Whoever says – that is, when he leaves

192 Reported by Imam Muslim in his *Sahih*: The Book on Remembrance, Supplications, Repentance and Forgiveness: The Chapter on Supplications: 17/202.

his home – *Bismillaah Tawakkaltu 'alaa Allah wa laa Haola walaa Quwwata illaa Billaah* (meaning: In the name of Allah, I place my reliance on Allah, and there is no power or might except with Allah), it will be said to him: 'You are sufficed and protected' and the Shaytaan withdraws from him."[193]

The Messenger of Allah ﷺ also said, "Were you to rely on Allah as it should be, you would have been provided for as the bird is provided for: it leaves in the morning, hungry, and returns in the night, full."[194]

The pious predecessors have encouraged relying on Allah and their lives express that:

- Imam Sa'eed bin Jubayr (d. 95 AH) would supplicate, saying, "O Allah, I ask You through reliance on You and thinking favourably about You." He would say, "Reliance on Allah is a gatherer of *Iman*."[195]

- It was said to Haatim al-Asamm (d. 237 AH), "Upon what did you base your affairs regarding *At-Tawakkul*?" He answered, "Upon four things: I recognize that my provision will not be eaten by other than me. So, I keep myself calm about it. I also recognize that my work will not be done by other than me. Thus, I am busy with it. I recognize that death will come suddenly. Hence, I get ahead of it. I

193 Reported by Imam At-Tirmidhi in his *Sunan*: The Book on Supplications: Chapter on What is Reported Regarding What it said when One Leaves his home: 5/490, and said concerning it: a *HasanSahih* Hadith.

194 The Hadith is reported by Imam At-Tirmidhi in his *Sunan*: The Book on Ascetics: The Chapter on Reliance on Allah, and said: a *HasanSahih* Hadith.

195 *Nuzhat ul-Fudaaa*: 1/393.

know that I cannot hide from Allah's Eye; so, I am shy of Him."[196]

- Ibn Abee Dunya (d. 281 AH) reported with his chain of transmission from Sa'eed bin Al-Musayyib ﷺ, who said, "Abdullah bin Salam and Salman ﷺ met and one of them said to the other, 'If you die before me, you should meet me and inform me of what you met with your Lord. And if I die before you, I will meet you and tell you.'

  So, one of them said to the other, 'Do the dead meet with the living?!' He replied, 'Yes, their souls go to wherever it likes in Paradise.' He said: Then, so-and-so died[197] and met him in his dream and then said: 'Rely on Allah and receive glad tidings. I never saw anything like reliance on Allah. Rely on Allah and receive glad tidings; I never saw anything like reliance on Allah."[198]

- Ibn Abee Dunya also reported with his chain of transmission from 'Awn bin Abdullah, who said: "While a man was in the city farmland during the tribulation of Abdullah bin Zubayr, reclining, holding something with which he scratched the ground, he suddenly raised his head and someone holding a spade came towards him. He said to him: 'O you, why are you reclining and sad?'" 'Awn said: "It was as if it debased him. So, he replied, 'Nothing.'" The owner of the spade then asked, 'Is it because of a worldly

196 The previous reference: 2/848.

197 It was Salman Al-Farsi ﷺ as mentioned by *Ustadh* Jaasim Al-Fuhayd in his editing of the book by Ibn Abee Dunya: *At-Tawakkul* in which this narration is reported.

198 The chain of transmission of this story is authentic as explained by the editor mentioned earlier; see the previous reference: pg. 63-64.

affair? This world is only passing; both the pious and the unrighteous partake in it but the hereafter is an appointed term when the Able Sovereign will separate between the truth and falsehood…' When the man heard that from him, as if astonished by what he heard, he said, 'Because of the present condition of the Muslims.'

The spade-man then remarked, 'Allah – the Mighty and Sublime – will save you by your sympathy for the Muslims. Supplicate, for no one asked and begged Allah – the Mighty and Sublime – except that He answered and granted him. No one relied on Him or trusted in Him except that He sufficed and saved him. The man said, 'So, I supplicated, O Allah, protect and save from me, and it (i.e. the tribulation) ended and I did not hit anyone."[199]

- Similarly, Ibn Abee Dunya reported with his chain of transmission from Wuhayb bin Al-Ward (d. 153 AH) that, "Two men had (their canoe) broken while on the sea and they both found themselves on the land. So, they came to a house built from wood and stayed inside it. One night, while one of them was asleep and the other awake, two women came and stood by the door. Their look was so disgusting to an extent known only to Allah – the Mighty and Sublime. So, one of the women said to the other, 'Go in', and she said, 'Woe to you, I can not.' She retorted, 'Woe to you, why?' She answered, 'Do you not see what is at the door?' There was a slate in the house with the inscription, 'Allah is sufficient for me and

199 The chain of transmission of this story is *Sahih* (authentic); see the last reference: pg. 67-68.

that is enough, Allah Hears the one who supplicates and there is no objective after Allah.'"[200]

9.3 Levels of *At-Tawakkul*

Reliance on Allah has categories based on the one relying on Allah, the strength of his *Iman*, and his determination:

1. **The First Level:** Knowing the Lord and His Attributes - His Ability, Sufficiency, non-dependence on anything, that all affairs are known to Him and that they are from His Will and Power. This recognition is the first step the servant takes regarding reliance on Allah.

2. **The Second Level:** Affirmation of the means[201] and the causes.

3. **The Third Level:** The Heart's firmness in the aspects of Allah's oneness regarding reliance.

4. **The Fourth Level**: The Heart's dependence on Allah, it's trusting and finding tranquillity in Him. This will be known from the fact that he will not bother about the ups and downs of the world, and his heart will not be disrurbed or throbbed when he loses what he likes or when something he dislikes happens to him. This is because the Heart's dependence is upon Allah with His tranquillity and trust. He had protected it from fear and worry.

200 In *Hilyat ul-Awliyaa*: It's end

201 They are the things Allah has subjected to us in the universe for use to ease our affairs; detailed explanation about that will come soon due to its importance and the difference amongst the people regarding it.

5. **The Fifth level:** Thinking favourably about Allah – the Mighty and Sublime – for to the extent of one's favourable thoughts about Allah and hope, is the reliance on Him.

6. **The Sixth Level:** Submitting the heart to Him together with its needs and cutting off its disputations.

7. **The Seventh level:** Entrusting: and it is the essence of reliance on Allah. That is, a person's leaving and placing all his affairs with Allah out of willingness, not out of grudge or coercion. The one who entrusts his affairs to Allah only does so because he desires that his affairs are better discharged for him, and even if what is done for him is different from what he thinks is good, he is pleased with it since he recognizes that it is better for him even when the benefits may not be clear to him (at the moment).[202]

Many of those who place reliance are held down in their reliance like the one who turns his reliance to something trivial, he puts in all his power of reliance while it is possible that he achieves it with the least thing and by making the heart rely on Allah regarding increase in *Eeman* and knowledge, helping the religion and positively impacting the world. This is the reliance of the weak and undetermined.

Some turn their determination and reliance and supplication towards an ailment which could be cured with the least thing or hunger which could be satisfied with half of a loaf or half of a *Dirham* and he abandons turning it towards helping the religion, restraining the innovators, increasing in *Iman* and things that benefit the Muslims.

The condition of the Prophet ﷺ and that of his companions

---

202 *Tahdheeb Madaarij is-Saalikeen*: pg. 337-341, with modification.

رضي الله عنهم is the standard condition and the measure, with which the right and wrong is recognized. Their determination regarding reliance on Allah was higher than that of those who came after them. Their reliance was about winning hearts and that Allah be worshipped in all the lands. So, they gained victory over the lands of the non-Muslims and made them lands of *Iman* (belief) and the breeze of the breath of life of reliance blew in the lives of their followers and thus, they filled the lands with *Yaqeen* (Certainty) and *Iman* (faith)."[203]

9.4 The Connection between *At-Tawakkul* and Means

It is an extremely important matter regarding which some have erred. However, the successful conformed with the truth. Some have completely abandoned the means, determining never to be deceived by it! Such were many among those who came before us and are few these days.

Others rely so much on the means to such an extent that they believe they cannot do without it. For them, life cannot be without it and that they will be destroyed if they don't depend on it. in all of this, they forget Allah to such an extent that the *Shaytaan* becomes pleased – And the refuge is with Allah! There are many such persons these days. The idea is common and deep-rooted in the minds of the people!

They are invited day and night with strong cravings, greed, and fear of the gloomy future – in their view. The successful one – in their erroneous view – is the one who gains from the worldly matters from which he can take care of himself

203 *Tahdheeb Madaarij is-Saalikeen*: pg. 343-344.

and his children and grand children to the level Allah Wills. So, for most of the people, the means become something worshipped together with Allah or asides Him. Only a few of them maintain a middle course, understand the means and its connection with the life of the Muslim in the right manner.

9.5 Regarding Those Who Completely Reject Means

You should know that those who reject the means have not established reliance on Allah at all because reliance on Allah is from the strongest means to attaining the objective. It is like supplication that Allah has made a means to achieve the request. If the servant believes that Allah has not made reliance a means or his supplications a means to the attainment of anything, then, he is seriously mistaken.

This is because Allah (the Exalted) has destined that one becomes full when he eats and satisfied when he drinks. If he does not do that, he does not get filled or satisfied. He also destined that one gets to Makkah and makes the pilgrimage when he travels but if he sits in his house he does not get to Makkah.

Therefore, compare what the rejecters of means say by abandoning all of these linking means, claiming that: if being full, satisfied or performing the pilgrimage and things like that were predestined for me it will surely get to me whether I move or not, travel or not. And that if they were not predestined for me it will not get to me whether I did anything or not! Will anyone consider such a person (with such thoughts) reasonable? Aren't the beasts more reasonable than him? Even the beasts seek means by basic intuition!

Even, to deny the means is irreconcilable with sound intellect, the *Sharee'ah* and sense. The Prophet ﷺ never contradicted means; he wore two armors on the day of (the battle of) Uhud and never came to the battle line unprotected as some of those without knowledge do. He also hired a polytheist road-guide who was upon the religion of his people to take him through the road while migrating. He would store a year's food for his family while he is the leader of those who rely on Allah. When he goes on expedition or pilgrimage or the lesser pilgrimage, he would take along provision..."[204]

As such, reliance on Allah "does not contradict seeking means upon which Allah has placed the order of this universe, by which He executed His orders. His Predestinations are established and His rulings are dispensed (through means)."[205] "The popular Hadith reported by Anas bin Maalik رضي الله عنه is evidence for that: He said, 'A man came on his ride and said, *O Messenger of Allah, should I fetter it (i.e. his beast) and then place reliance (on Allah)? Or, I should leave it loose and then place reliance?* He ﷺ said, *Fetter it and place reliance (on Allah).*' This is a clear-cut conclusive text, regarding seeking means, and that doing so does not contradict reliance on Allah."[206]

How beautiful is this saying of the poet:

> Rely on the most-Merciful in every affair
>
> Do not desire frailty any day away from seeking
>
> Do you not consider that Allah said to Maryam?

---

204 *Tahdheeb Madaarij is-Saalikeen*: pg. 338-339.
205 *At-Tawakkul* by *Ustadh* Yusuf Al-Qaradawi: pg. 35.
206 *At-Tawakkul*: pg. 35.

'And shake the trunk of date-palm towards you, the fresh dates will fall'

If He willed that she plucked it without any shaking

She would pluck it, but everything has means!

Ustadh Al-Qaradawi said: "The fact is that those who reject the means completely have no evidence from the Qur'aan or *Sunnah* or from the actions of the companions and those who followed them in goodness...If the Muslims in the best of generations were upon this methodology (of complete rejection of means), their religion will not be assisted for them, no civilization will be found for them and no sovereignty will be established for them anywhere. This negative disposition (i.e. the idea of complete rejection of means) is strange to the Islamic mentality, spirit and methodology which are employed to bring about a righteous personality, family and community. Therefore, the established, reliable, model scholars of jurisprudence in the *Ummah* reject it.

Imam Sufyan bin Sa'eed Ath-Thaoree – a leading scholar of jurisprudence, Hadith, and ascetics says: 'When a scholar does not have a means of livelihood, he becomes an agent of the tyrants. When the servant has no means of livelihood he gives his religion for food. And when the ignorant has no means of livelihood, he becomes an agent of evil-doers.'"[207]

"Ibn Jawzee ﷀ said: This (complete rejection of means) is the view of those who do not understand the essence of reliance on Allah. So, they think that it is leaving earning and not making the limbs do anything. We had explained that reliance on Allah is an action of the heart and as such, does not contradict those of the limbs. If everyone who earns

207 The last reference: pg. 46.

becomes non-reliant on Allah (by so doing), the Prophets would have been considered so too! Adam – peace be upon him – was a plowman, Nuh and Zakariyyah were both carpenters, Idrees was a tailor, Loot and Ibraaheem were both farmers, Saalih was a merchant, Sulayman weaved, Dawud made armor and ate from his earnings, Musa, Shu'ayb, Muhammad were shepherds – may the peace and blessings of Allah be upon them all."[208]

9.6 Refuting Those Who only Depend on Means

They are upon something very dangerous due to their forgetting Allah the Mighty and Sublime and their completely turning towards the means.

The means is only dispraised - in this case - "when the heart becomes attached to it alone and places all of its dependence on it forgetting its Causer and Creator. Such a person knows not that the means do not act alone. The Qur'aan has mentioned to us some examples of relying upon the physical means alone, that it does not actually bring about success and that is in His saying:

لَقَدْ نَصَرَكُمُ ٱللَّهُ فِي مَوَاطِنَ كَثِيرَةٍ وَيَوْمَ حُنَيْنٍ إِذْ أَعْجَبَتْكُمْ كَثْرَتُكُمْ فَلَمْ تُغْنِ
عَنكُمْ شَيْـًٔا وَضَاقَتْ عَلَيْكُمُ ٱلْأَرْضُ بِمَا رَحُبَتْ ثُمَّ وَلَّيْتُم مُّدْبِرِينَ ﴿٢٥﴾

«Truly Allah has given you victory on many battle fields, and on the Day of *Hunayn* (battle) when you rejoiced at your great number but it availed you

---

208 *At-Tawakkul*: pg. 51.

naught and the earth, vast as it is, was straitened for you, then you turned back in flight.»

At-Tawbah (Q9:25)

They were disappointed while they had great number because their number made them feel such that they should not. It got them busy away from reliance on Allah but did not avail anything. This is as against when they were assisted while they had small number when their dependence was upon Allah alone after they had put in their own utmost."[209]

The middle-course between these two extremes – rejecting means completely and depending solely on it - is that of the person who seeks the means while truly relying on Allah. "So, he is with the means by his limbs and all of his body and with his Lord with his intellect and mind. He is the one who has kept the way of Allah over His creatures, His rulings over them, being certain that Allah (the Exalted) placed the means, commanded following it and placed upon it, its impacts out of His Predestination and Ruling and He is the one – at the same time – who can stop it if He Willed, and that He could create impediments that will hinder its movement or destroy its impacts."[210]

9.7 Some Benefits of Reliance on Allah

Placing reliance on Allah has great benefits from which are: tranquillity, peace of mind, power, honour, pleasure, hope; and each of these benefits has things pointing to it and narrations which I have left for brevity."[211]

209 The last reference: pg. 65
210 *At-Tawakkul*: pg. 73.
211 See the last reference: 95 – 107.

9.8 Things that Aid *At-Tawakkul*

They are many; such as: knowing Allah (the Exalted) by His Beautiful Names and Exalted Attributes, trusting in Allah the Mighty and Sublime, knowing that man is incapable and weak, recognizing the virtues of relying on Allah and its importance. And every aid mentioned here has corroborating narrations which I have left for brevity.[212]

9.9 Things that Hinder *At-Tawakkul*

From that is: not knowing Allah (the Exalted) and His Greatness, self-deception, depending on creatures, love of this world and being deceived by it.[213]

9.10 Basic Rules and Words of Advice

1. *At-Tawakkul* is the Heart's worship with the greatest connection with the Beautiful Names of Allah:

"It has connection with the Name, *Al-Gaffaar* (The Oft-Forgiving), *At-Tawwaab* (The One Who Accepts Repentance), *Al-'Afuww* (The One Who Overlooks), *Ar-Rauf* (The Kind), *Ar-Raheem* (The most-Merciful). It is also connected with the Name: *Al-Fattaah* (The Victor), *Al-Wahhaab* (The Provider), *Ar-Razzaaq* (The One Who Enriches), *Al-Mu'tee* (The Giver), *Al-Muhsin* (The Benefactor).

It is connected again with *Al-Mu'izz* (The Granter of

212 See the last reference: pg. 106 – 108.
213 See the last reference: pg. 117-125.

Honour), *Al-Mudhill* (The One Who Humbles), *Al-Khaafid* (The One Who Lowers), *Ar-Raafi'* (The One Who Raises), *Al-Maani'* (The One Who Prevents) from the angle of his reliance on Him to disgrace the enemies of His religion, abase them and denying them the means of victory.

It is also has connection with His Attributes: *Al-Qudrah* (Ability) and *Al-Iraadah* (Wish)

It also has general connection with the all the Beautiful Names and thus, it (*Tawakkul*) is described - by some as knowing Allah".[214]

2. *At-Tawakkul* does not negate Seeking Cure:

It is contained in the authentic Hadith from the Prophet ﷺ regarding the attributes of the seventy thousand people who will enter Paradise without accounting that they are: "those who do not seek *Ruqya*, do not take to evil omen or do cauterization. They rely upon their Lord."[215] It may be understood from this Hadith is that seeking cure by *Ruqya* and cauterization contradicts reliance on Allah.

However, many of the leading scholars have explained this Hadith, harmonizing it with the narrations which inform about the prophet's seeking cure and his command to his companions to seek cure.

From those explanations are:

i. This particular Hadith only refers to those who avoid that (i.e. *Ruqya* and cauterization) when they are

---

214 *Tahdheeb Madaarij is-Saalikeen*: pg. 343

215 Reported by Imam Bukhaari in is *Sahih*: The Book on Medicine: The Chapter on the one who will not seek *Ruqya*.

healthy fearing illness. But whoever takes medicine while ill, then the Hadith does not apply to them.

ii. It could mean that those mentioned in the Hadith are those who know not about the affairs of this world and its means of preventing these contingencies. So, they do not know cauterization or the use of *Ruqya*, and do not have any way-out of what comes upon them except supplication and depending on Allah, being pleased with His decrees. They have passed by Medicine and doctors, *Ruqya* and those who administer it, but and have not the knowledge of any of that.

iii. What leaving *Ruqya* and cauterization means is relying on Allah to remove illness, and being pleased with His decrees and not a negation of the permissibility of that since these things are established in authentic narrations and from the pious predecessors. However, the status of pleasure and submission is greater than following the means.[216]

"*Ruqya* is established (to be allowed or even encouraged) from the sayings of the Prophet ﷺ, his actions and approvals, and known formulas of *Ruqya* have been reported from him. Imam Ibn Taimiyyah رحمه الله has mentioned that what is rejected (i.e. about seeking *Ruqya* etc. in the Hadith) is seeking *Ruqya* (to be administered on one) and not *Ruqya* itself."

It could also be said that the Hadith does not mean that the seventy thousand are the only people who place reliance on Allah, but that they are a distinct group, and as such, their

216 *At-Tawakkul* by Dr. Yusuf Al-Qaradawi: pg. 85. With some modification.

conducts are better and not necessarily that it is a condition (for *Tawakkul*).[217]

9.11 Seeking Allah's Guidance is from the Forms of *At-Tawakkul*

The one who seeks to be guided by Allah relies on Him concerning differenciating good from evil, the beneficial from the harmful, and submits to Him in all of that completely. And Allah knows Best.

217 The last reference: pg. 88.

Chapter 10

Al-Khawf (Being Afraid of Allah - the Exalted)

It is from the most beneficial of the heart-related acts of worship due to its great influence on the conduct of the Muslim and his intentions. It is "the Heart's aching and intense feeling due to its anticipation of something unpleasant in the future."[218]

Allah the Mighty and Sublime said:

... فَلَا تَخَافُوهُمْ وَخَافُونِ إِن كُنتُم مُّؤْمِنِينَ ﴿١٧٥﴾

«So fear them not, but fear Me, if you are (true) believers.»

Aal Imran (Q3:175)

And He said:

.... وَإِيَّايَ فَارْهَبُونِ ﴿٤٠﴾

218 *Ithaaf us-Saadaat il-Muttaqeen*: 11/383.

«And fear none but Me.»

Al-Baqarah (Q2:40)

He the Mighty and Sublime said:

إِنَّ ٱلَّذِينَ هُم مِّنْ خَشْيَةِ رَبِّهِم مُّشْفِقُونَ ﴿٥٧﴾ وَٱلَّذِينَ هُم بِـَٔايَٰتِ رَبِّهِمْ
يُؤْمِنُونَ ﴿٥٨﴾ وَٱلَّذِينَ هُم بِرَبِّهِمْ لَا يُشْرِكُونَ ﴿٥٩﴾ وَٱلَّذِينَ يُؤْتُونَ مَآ ءَاتَوا۟ وَّقُلُوبُهُمْ
وَجِلَةٌ أَنَّهُمْ إِلَىٰ رَبِّهِمْ رَٰجِعُونَ ﴿٦٠﴾ أُو۟لَٰٓئِكَ يُسَٰرِعُونَ فِى ٱلْخَيْرَٰتِ وَهُمْ لَهَا
سَٰبِقُونَ ﴿٦١﴾

«Verily! Those who live in awe for fear of their Lord. And those who believe in the *Ayaat* (proofs, evidences, verses, lessons, signs, revelations, etc.) of their Lord. And those who join not anyone (in worship) as partners with their Lord. And those who give that (their charity) which they give (and also do other good deeds) with their hearts full of fear (whether their alms and charities, etc., have been accepted or not), because they are sure to return to their Lord (for reckoning).It is these who race for the good deeds, and they are foremost in them [e.g. offering the compulsory *Salah* (prayers) in their (early) stated, fixed times and so on].»

Al-Mu'minun:(Q23: 57-61)

And the mother of the believers, Aa'isha رضي الله عنها (may Allah be pleased with her) said, 'O Messenger of Allah ﷺ in this verse,

وَٱلَّذِينَ يُؤْتُونَ مَآ ءَاتَوا۟ و ... ﴿٦٠﴾

«And those who give that (their charity) which they give.»

Al-Mu'minun:(Q23:60)

Is it regarding the one who steals, commits illicit intercourse and consumes alcohol? He said: 'No, O daughter of Abu Bakr, O daughter of As-Siddeeq! It is regarding the one who performs the prayers, fasts and gives charity while being afraid of Allah – the Mighty and Exalted.'"[219]

Al-Hasan Al-Basree said regarding this verse: "By Allah, they engaged in good deeds, strove regarding it and feared that it be rejected. The believer combines goodness and fear, but the hypocrite combines evil and security!".[220]

Khashyah (Reverence) and *Khawf* (Fear) have similar meanings, but reverence is more special than fear because reverence is for the learned about Allah. Allah – Glorious is He – said,

.... إِنَّمَا يَخْشَى ٱللَّهَ مِنْ عِبَادِهِ ٱلْعُلَمَـٰٓؤُا۟ ۗ إِنَّ ٱللَّهَ عَزِيزٌ غَفُورٌ ﴿٢٨﴾

«It is only those who have knowledge among His slaves that revere Allah.»

Faatir (Q35:28)

219 Reported by Imam Ahmad in his *Musnad*, its chain of transmission is *Sahih* (authentic). See *Fath ur-Rabbaanee*: 18/ 216-217.

220 *Tahdheeb Madaarij is-Saalikeen*: pg. 269.

Thus, it is fear combined with knowing.[221]

Allah (the Exalted) also said:

وَأُزْلِفَتِ ٱلْجَنَّةُ لِلْمُتَّقِينَ غَيْرَ بَعِيدٍ ﴿٣١﴾ هَٰذَا مَا تُوعَدُونَ لِكُلِّ أَوَّابٍ
حَفِيظٍ ﴿٣٢﴾ مَّنْ خَشِيَ ٱلرَّحْمَٰنَ بِٱلْغَيْبِ وَجَآءَ بِقَلْبٍ مُّنِيبٍ ﴿٣٣﴾

«And Paradise will be brought near to the *Muttaqoon* (pious) not far off. (It will be said): 'This is what you were promised, - (it is) for those oft-returning (to Allah) in sincere repentance, and those who preserve their covenant with Allah (by obeying Him in all what He has ordered, and worship none but Allah Alone)'. Who feared the Most Beneficent (Allah) in the *Ghayb* (unseen): (i.e. in this worldly life before seeing and meeting Him), and brought a heart turned in repentance (to Him - and absolutely free from each and every kind of polytheism).»

Qaaf (Q50:31-33)

10.1 The Excellence of Weeping Out of Fear of Allah and Reverence for Him

Abu Hurayrah رضي الله عنه said, "The Prophet ﷺ said, 'A man who weeps out of the fear of Allah will not enter the Fire until milk returns to the udders…'"[222]

- When Muhammad bin Al-Munkadir (d. 130 AH)

221 See the last reference.

222 Reported by Imam At-Tirmidhi in his *Sunan*: The Book on Ascetics: The Chapter on What is Reported about Weeping from the Fear of Allah: 4/ 555, and said regarding it; *HasanSahih*.

weeps, he wipes his face and beard of his tears and says: "I was informed that the Fire will not touch the spot touched by the tears."

- Ka'b Al-Ahbaar رضي الله عنه said, "That I weep out of reverence for Allah is more beloved to me than that I give two measures of gold in charity."[223]

10.2 Some Statements of the Salaf on Fear

- Fear is the whip of Allah with which He rectifies those who leave His path.

- When fear becomes established in a heart, it burns the spots of destructive desires in it and throws worldliness out of it.

- True fear of Allah is abstinence from sins, openly and secretly.

- The praise-worthy fear of Allah is that which restrains you from Allah's prohibitions.[224]

- It is not the one who weeps and wipes his face that actually fears Allah, rather, the one who abstains from what he fears being punished for.[225]

- Whoever fears Allah, no one will harm him; but whoever fears other than Allah, no one will benefit him.[226]

223 *Nuzhat ul-Fudalaa*: 1/496.
224 The last number of statements was quoted from: *Tahdheeb Madaarij is-Saalikeen*: pg. 270-271.
225 *Ithaaf Saadat il-Muttaqeen*: 11/387.
226 *Nuzhat ul-Fudalaa*: 2/661

- A servant does not seek aid for his religion with anything as great as reverence for Allah.

10.3 What the Pious Servant Fears

The pious servant fears falling into *Kufr* (disbelief) and *Nifaaq* (hypocrisy).

1. He fears an evil end for himself.

2. He fears falling into sins.

3. He fears dying before repenting.

4. He fears contravening repentance and breaking covenant with Allah.

5. He fears being granted abundant favour while upon sins.

6. He fears being deceived by the allurements of this world.[227]

10.4 The Prophet's Apprehension Over His Ummah and the Fear of the Pious

Anas رضي الله عنه said, "The Messenger of Allah ﷺ gave a sermon the like of which I have never heard. He said, 'If you were to know what I know, you will laugh only a little and weep much."[228]

227 *Ithaaf Saadat il-Muttaqeen*: 11/398-399.

228 Reported by Imam Al-Bukhaari in his *Sahih*: The Book on Mind-Softeners: The Chapter on The Prophet's Saying; 'If you were to know what I know, you will laugh only a little and weep much': 7/126.

Aa'isha ﷺ reported that Allah's Messenger ﷺ, "When he saw a cloud or it becomes windy it would be noticed on his face." She said, "O Messenger of Allah, when the people see the clouds, they become happy expecting that it rains, but I find that when you see them, dislike is noticed on your face. So, he ﷺ said: 'O Aa'isha, do you not believe that it could contain punishment? Some people were destroyed with the wind and some people saw the punishment and said: *This is a cloud bringing us rain.*'"[229]

When he ﷺ enters the prayer, his heart is heard to hum like the humming of a boiler.[230]

- Al-Hasan Al-Basree said, "Umar would recite a verse during his regular supplications and the lesson it contains chokes him. So, he would cry until he falls down. He then keeps to his house until he is visited (by people) thinking that he was ill."[231]

- Once, he passed by the house of a person while he was praying and reciting *Surah At-Tur*. He stood listening and when he reached His saying:

إِنَّ عَذَابَ رَبِّكَ لَوَاقِعٌ ۝٧ مَّا لَهُۥ مِن دَافِعٍ ۝٨

229 Reported by Imam Al-Bukhaari in the Book of *Tafseer*: The *Tafseer* of *Soorah Al-Ahqaaf*: 7/126.

230 Reported by Imam At-Tirmidhi in *Ash-Shamaail*: Chapter on what is Reported about the Weeping of the Prophet ﷺ : 255, with a chain of reliable narrators.

231 *Ithaaf Saadat il-Muttaqeen*: 11/490.

«Verily, the Torment of your Lord will surely come to pass. There is none that can avert it».

At-Tur (Q52:7-8)

He came down from his donkey, leaned on a wall, and stayed for sometime. He returned to his house and took ill for a month. People visited him not knowing what caused his illness."[232]

- One day, Ali ﵁ finished the Morning Prayer while he was very worried. He said, while waving his hand, "I had seen the companions of Muhammad ﷺ, but I cannot see anything like their's today. They would wake up in the morning, disheveled, hungry, dusty with coarseness seen on their faces. They would have spent the night in prostration and standing and reciting Allah's Book, changing the positions of their prostrations and feet. When it is morning, they would remember Allah, shaking as the tree shakes on a windy day. Tears fill their eyes until their clothes become wet. By Allah, it was as if I passed the night with the people (of this time) while they are heedless." Then he stood up and was not seen after that laughing until Ibn Muljam stabbed him.[233]

- Muhammad bin Al-Munkadir (d. 130 AH) stood up one night to pray and he started to weep. He wept so much that his household feared for him. They asked him but could not understand anything from him while he continued to cry. So they sent for Abu Haazim Salamah bin Deenaar (d. 140 AH) who came to him and said, "What makes you weep?"

232 The last reference: 11/490.
233 *Ithaaf Saadat il-Muttaqeen*: 11/491.

He replied, "I came across a verse." He asked what it was. He answered,

.... وَبَدَا لَهُم مِّنَ ٱللَّهِ مَا لَمْ يَكُونُوا۟ يَحْتَسِبُونَ ﴿٤٧﴾

«And there will become apparent to them from Allah, what they had not been reckoning.»

Az-Zumar (Q39:47)

Abu Haazim also started to weep and they both wept profusely.[234]

- 'Ataa Al-Khaffaaf said, "I never met Sufyaan Ath-Thaoree except that he was weeping." So, I said (to him), 'What has happened to you?' He said, 'I am afraid of being written in the Mother of The Book as wretched.'"[235]

- Abu Abdir-Rahmaan Al-Asadee said, "I said to Sa'eed bin Abdul-'Azeez (d. 167 AH), 'Why do you weep during the prayer.' He replied, 'O my cousin, why did you ask regarding that?' I said, 'Perhaps Allah may make it benefit me.' Then he remarked, 'I never stood up for the prayers except that the Hell is depicted to me!'"[236]

- Maalik bin Deenaar (d. 127 AH) said, "While I was circumambulating the house (the Ka'bah), suddenly I came near a worshipping young lady holding the covering of the Ka'bah and saying, 'O Allah, how

234 *Nuzhat ul-Fudalaa*: 1/495.
235 The last reference: 2/586.
236 The last reference: 2/611.

much of desires lost its sweetness remaining its defects? O Allah! Don't You have punishments other than the Fire?' She continued to weep and she was in that condition until dawn."

Maalik went on, "When I saw that, I placed my hand on my head and said aloud, 'The mother of Maalik has lost him.'"[237]

- And Nu'aym bin Hammaad (d. 229 AH) said, "When Ibn Mubarak (d. 181 AH) reads any book on mind-softening, he becomes like a slaughtered bull or cow due to excessive weeping. No one amongst us was bold enough to ask him a question except that he warded it off."[238]

- Imam At-Tirmidhi (d. 279 AH) cried until he turned blind and cried for years as a blind.[239]

- And this was *Shaykh al-Islam*, Abdullah bin Wahb Al-Misree, the great scholar of Hadith: one of his books – *Ahwaal ul-Qiyaamah* (The Difficulties of the Judgment Day) was read to him. He fell (on the ground being) unconscious and never spoke a word until he died few days later – may Allah, the most High shower blessings on him.[240]

- Imam Ash-Shafi'i was with Sufyaan bin 'Uyaynah

237 *Ithaaf Saadat il-Muttaqeen*: 11/493-494. "An expression used by the Arabs to show abhorrence not intending its actual meaning." *Fath ul-Baaree*: 11/486. **(TN)**

238 *Nuzhat ul-Fudalaa: 2/ 655.*

239 *The last reference: 2/969.*

240 The last reference: 2/707.

and the latter narrated a mind-softening Hadith and Ash-Shafi'i became unconscious.[241]

- This was Ali bin Fudayl bin 'Iyyaad – he was from the eminent and pious reliable people. He died due to a verse he heard, and that was Allah's saying:

وَلَوْ تَرَىٰٓ إِذْ وُقِفُوا۟ عَلَى ٱلنَّارِ فَقَالُوا۟ يَٰلَيْتَنَا نُرَدُّ ... ﴿٢٧﴾

If you could but see when they will be held over the (Hell) Fire! They will say: 'Would that we were but sent back (to the world)!'»[242]

Al-An'am (Q6:27)

- When Sufyan At-Thawri ﵀ speaks about remembering the Last Day he passes blood.[243]

- Abu Hurayrah ﵁ who said that the Prophet ﷺ said, "There was a man who lost hopes regarding his deeds. When he was about to die, he said to his children, 'When I am dead, burn me, then grind me to ashes and then disperse me in the wind. For by Allah, if my Lord gets me, he will punish me in a manner He has never punished anyone.' When he died, that was done to him and Allah commanded the earth and said, 'Put together what is inside you'. So it did and here he was standing. He said: 'What led you to what

241 The last reference: 2/734.
242 The last reference: 2/669.
243 The last reference: 2/584.

you did?' He said, 'O Lord, Your reverence!' And he was forgiven."[244]

10.5 Praise-worthy and Encouraged Fear

The true, praise-worthy fear is that which puts a person away from the prohibitions of Allah the Mighty and Sublime. When it exceeds that, hopelessness is feared from it."[245] "The heart in its journey towards Allah – the Mighty and Sublime, has being afraid of Allah (the Exalted) and hope are like its two wings. For when the head and the wings are sound, the bird flies well, but when the head is cut-off, the bird dies. And when the two wings are missing, it becomes a target for every hunter and prey."[246]

The fear of Allah is connected with hope in a manner to be explained – Allah Willing – in the next heart-based act of worship.

244 Reported by Imam Al-Bukhaari in his *Sahih*: The Book on the Narrations from the Prophets ﷺ: The Chapter on What is Reported from the Children of Israaeel: 4/214-215

245 *Tahdheeb Madaarij is-Saalikeen*: pg. 270

246 The last reference: pg. 272

Chapter 11
Ar-Rajaa (Hope in Allah)

It is "being joyful at the generosity and favour of the Lord the Mighty and Sublime and being satisfied with looking forward to His bounties." It is said, "It is trusting in the generosity of the Lord – (the Exalted)."[247]

11.1 Forms of Hope in Allah

1. The first form

The hope of a person who acts in obedience to Allah through His guidance. Such a person hopes for to His reward.

2. The second form

A person who commits a sin and then repents from it. He is hopeful of Allah's forgiveness, pardon, generosity, mercy and favour.

3. The third form

A person who persists upon negligence and disobedience

247 *Tahdheeb Madaarij is-Saalikeen*: pg. 297.

while looking forward to the mercy of Allah without (appropriate) action.

As for the first two forms, they are both praise-worthy, but for the third, it is deception and false desire and hope.[248] Allah (the Exalted),

.... فَمَن كَانَ يَرْجُوا۟ لِقَآءَ رَبِّهِۦ فَلْيَعْمَلْ عَمَلًا صَٰلِحًا وَلَا يُشْرِكْ بِعِبَادَةِ رَبِّهِۦٓ أَحَدًۢا ﴿١١٠﴾

«So whoever hopes for the Meeting with his Lord, let him work righteousness and associate none as a partner in the worship of his Lord.»

Al-Kahf (Q18:110)

There are many Hadith narrations regarding *Ar-Rajaa* (Hope in Allah) and its virtues such as:

Anas ﷺ said, "I heard Allah's Messenger ﷺ saying, 'Allah the Mighty and Sublime said, 'O son of Adam, as long as you beseech me and hope in me, I will forgive you no matter what you have (of sins) and I am unconcerned. O son of Adam, were your sins to reach the clouds of the sky and then you seek forgiveness from me, I will forgive you and I am unconcerned. O son of Adam, if you were to come to me with what almost fills the earth of sins and then, you meet Me, not joining anything in partnership with Me, I will give you what almost fills it (the earth) of forgiveness.'"[249]

248 The last reference: with modification.

249 Reported by Imam At-Tirmidhi in his *Sunan*: The Chapters on Supplications from Allah's Messenger ﷺ : The Chapter on What is reported on The Virtues of Repentance and Forgiveness and What is Mentioned Regarding Allah's Mercy over His Servants: 5/548; and said about it: A *Gareeb* Hadith, and it is a *Hasan* Hadith.

Similarly, Abu Hurayrah ﷺ reported from Allah's Messenger ﷺ that, "Allah – the Mighty and Sublime – said, 'I am (able to do) for My servant what he thinks of Me…"[250]

11.2 The Status of *Ar-Rajaa*

Ar-Rajaa is from the highest, most lofty and honourable status. It is the pivot of the path to complete devotion to Allah, together with loving Allah and fearing him. Were it not for the feeling of *Ar-Rajaa* (hope), the Heart's worship and that of the other limbs will be thwarted. Even, were it not for *Ar-Rajaa* (hope), it would not have moved in obedience…"[251]

Every Muslim needs to be hopeful, so, "he moves between a sin which he hopes will be forgiven, an imperfection which he hopes to rectify, a good deed which he hopes is accepted, steadfastness which he hopes to attain and sustain, getting closer to Allah and a status before Him which he hopes to reach…"[252]

Some of what *Ar-Rajaa* prevents:

1. Prevention of great fear; and its explanation will soon follow.

2. *Ar-Rajaa* makes the path to complete devotion to Allah pleasant and encourages the hopeful upon it.

250 Reported by Imam Al-Bukhaari in his *Sahih*: the Book on The Oneness of Allah: Chapter on What is Reported About the Essence, Attributes and Names of Allah: 9/147.

251 *Tahdheeb Madaarij is-Saalikeen*: pg. 298-299.

252 The last reference: pg. 300

3. Ar-*Rajaa* includes waiting and looking forward to Allah's favour. This makes the heart regularly connected to the remembrance of Allah and regularly gives consideration to His Names and Attributes.[253]

11.3 Connection between Hope and Fear

Fear is a whip with which Allah the Mighty and Sublime disciplines His servant. On the other hand, the hope (in Him) brings him ease so that it (the fear) does not drive the believer into hopelessness.

The pious predecessors have encouraged the Muslim to make the fear stronger than hope when he is healthy until his affairs become right and he keeps away from sins. However, when death approaches him, he should strengthen the aspect of hope in Allah's mercy and His pardon. Jaabir رضي الله عنه said that he heard the Prophet ﷺ, three days before his death, saying, 'No one of you should die except that he is thinking favourably about Allah – the Mighty and Sublime.'"[254]

Anas رضي الله عنه said that the Prophet ﷺ visited a young man while he was passing away and said, "How have I found you?" He answered, "O Messenger of Allah, I hope in Allah and fear because of my sins." Then, Allah's Messenger ﷺ said, "These two do not combine in the heart of a servant in the like of this circumstance except that Allah grants him what he hopes for and protects him from what he fears."[255]

253 The last reference: pg. 302 – 304 with modification.

254 Reported by Imam Muslim in his *Sahih*: The Book on Paradise, Its Enjoyments and People: the Chapter on the Order to think Favourably about Allah when Death Approaches: 8/329.

255 Reported by Imam At-Tirmidhi in his *Sunan*: The Book on Funerals 3/113; and said about it: *Hasan Gareeb*. Haafidh Al-Mundhiree had graded this Hadith *Hasan*. See: *At-Targeeb wat-Tarheeb*: 4/268.

Fudayl said: Fear is more virtuous than hope as long as the servant is healthy, but when death approaches him, then hope is better.[256]

The condition of some of the pious predecessors at death, when they grew more hopeful after being more afraid

- When death approached Bilal, his wife said: "We will grieve over him." He said, "You should rather say, *we will be joyous over him.* Tomorrow we will meet the beloved ones: Muhammad and his party.'"[257]

- While passing away, Mu'adh ﷺ said, "O Allah, I used to fear You, but today, I hope in you"[258]

- And this was Makhool Ash-Shaamee – from the eminent among the *Tabi'un* – he was always sad and was visited while ill before he died but was laughing. They spoke to him about that and he said: "Why should I not smile when I will soon leave the one I used to dread and arrive before the One I hope in and crave."[259]

- Abdullah bin Al-Mubarak (d. 181 AH) opened his eyes while passing away, laughed and said: "For the like of this let the workers work."[260]

---

256 *Nuzhat ul-Fudalaa*: 2/665..
257 *Ithaaf Saadaat il-Muttaqeen*: 14/208.
258 The last reference: 14/204.
259 The last reference: 14/219.
260 The last reference: 14/214.

[illegible] more than hope as long as the [illegible] healthy, but when death approaches [illegible] hope [illegible]

[illegible]

- When Bilal approached [illegible] his wife said, "[illegible]" [illegible] "[illegible] Tomorrow we will meet the [illegible] Muhammad and his party."

- When [illegible] Bilal [illegible]

- [illegible] Abdullah [illegible] from the [illegible]

- Abdullah [illegible] apart [illegible]

Chapter 12
Basic Noble Characters

After discussing some heart-based acts of worship which are the pivots of knowledge, I will discuss some of the characters that are greatly connected to the Heart's worship which the pious servant must exemplify. In fact, they may even be considered part of them.

Moreover, Sincerity, Reliance on Allah, Being afraid of Allah and Hoping in Him – which are all heart-based worship as discussed earlier - will not be considered true without the basic noble characters like *As-Sidq* (Trustfulness) in dealings and *Tawaadu'* (Humility) and others. This is because the rectification of the heart-based acts of worship is the foundation while noble characters form the building which reflects the strength of the foundation. So, what is in the heart of a slave, of turning towards his Lord, manifests in his conduct, character and methodology.

The following sections, dear Muslims, covers some of these desired basic characteristics and conduct.

12.1 *As-Sidq* (Truthfulness)

It is the Muslim's character and his defence. Whoever takes to it succeeds in this world and the hereafter, but whoever neglects it is disgraced before his death. He becomes so disgraced that he is unable to get out of it until the Day of Resurrection.

Allah the Mighty and Sublime has praised the truthful and commanded the Muslims to always be with them. He (the Exalted) said:

يَٰٓأَيُّهَا ٱلَّذِينَ ءَامَنُوا۟ ٱتَّقُوا۟ ٱللَّهَ وَكُونُوا۟ مَعَ ٱلصَّٰدِقِينَ ﴿١١٩﴾

«O you who believe! Be afraid of Allah, and be with those who are true (in words and deeds).»

At-Tawbah (Q9:119)

Allah – Glorious is He – classed people as: the truthful and the hypocrites. He (the Exalted) said:

لِّيَجْزِيَ ٱللَّهُ ٱلصَّٰدِقِينَ بِصِدْقِهِمْ وَيُعَذِّبَ ٱلْمُنَٰفِقِينَ إِن شَآءَ أَوْ يَتُوبَ عَلَيْهِمْ ۚ
إِنَّ ٱللَّهَ كَانَ غَفُورًا رَّحِيمًا ﴿٢٤﴾

«That Allah may reward the men of truth for their truth (i.e. for their patience at the accomplishment of that which they covenanted with Allah), and punish the hypocrites if He will or accept their repentance by turning to them in Mercy. Verily, Allah is Oft Forgiving, Most Merciful».

Al-Ahzab (Q33:24)

The foundation of *Iman* (faith) is *As-Sidq* (Truthfulness) while the basis of *Nifaaq* (hypocrisy) is falsehood. Allah (the Exalted) said that on the Day of Resurrection, nothing will benefit the servant and protect him from His punishment is his truthfulness – after Allah's *tawfeeq*. He (the Exalted) said,

... هَٰذَا يَوْمُ يَنفَعُ ٱلصَّٰدِقِينَ صِدْقُهُمْ ۚ لَهُمْ جَنَّٰتٌ تَجْرِي مِن تَحْتِهَا ٱلْأَنْهَٰرُ
خَٰلِدِينَ فِيهَآ أَبَدًا ۚ رَّضِيَ ٱللَّهُ عَنْهُمْ وَرَضُوا۟ عَنْهُ ۚ ذَٰلِكَ ٱلْفَوْزُ ٱلْعَظِيمُ ﴿١١٩﴾

«This is a Day on which the truthful will profit from their truth: theirs are Gardens under which rivers flow (in Paradise) - they shall abide therein forever. Allah is pleased with them and they with Him. That is the great success (Paradise).»

Al-Ma'idah (Q5:19)

He – Glorious is He – also said:

.... لَا يَهْدِي مَنْ هُوَ مُسْرِفٌ كَذَّابٌ ﴿٢٨﴾

«Verily, Allah guides not one who is a *Musrif* (a polytheist, or a murderer who shed blood without a right, or those who commit great sins, oppressor, transgressor), a liar!»

Ghafir (Q40:28)

—Virtues and Essence of *Sidq*

- It is the equality of the secret and open.
- And saying the truth in difficult situations.
- Saying the truth before someone you fear and look forward to.
- The essence of truthfulness is that you say the truth in situations where nothing – apparently – will salvage you except falsehood.[261]

It is said: Three things will not harm the truthful: sweet-talking, appearance, and awe.

It is also said: You will not find the truthful except while fulfilling an obligation or being involved in something beneficial.[262]

—Encouragement towards *Sidq* and Warning against Falsehood

Abu Umāma ﷺ that the Prophet ﷺ said, "I guarantee a castle around Paradise for the one who abandons arguments even while on the right; and a castle at the middle of Paradise for the one who leaves lying even while joking; and a castle in the loftiest parts of Paradise for the one who perfects his character."[263]

Hasan bin Ali ﷺ said, "I memorized from Allah's Messenger

261 And that is similar to the story of Ka'b bin Maalik ﷺ which had preceded under repentance.

262 See: *Tahdheeb Madaarij is-Saalikeen*: pg. 401.

263 Reported by Imam Abu Dawud in his *Sunan*: The Book on Conducts: The Chapter on Modesty.

ﷺ, "Leave that which makes you doubt for that which is free from doubt, for truth is soothing and falsehood is bothering."[264]

Ibn Mas'ood رضي الله عنه said, "The Messenger of Allah ﷺ said, 'Certainly, truth guides to virtue and virtue guides to Paradise. A man will persist telling the truth till he is named Truthful before Allah. Falsehood leads to vice and vice leads to the Fire; and a man persists telling lies till he is named Liar before Allah."[265]

The Prophet ﷺ narrated what he witnessed of the punishment of the liars, and said, "I saw two men this night who both approached me..." He then said, "...as for the one you saw his cheeks being pierced, he is the liar who tells lies and it will be transmitted from him until it gets to distant regions. He will be dealt with like that till the Day of Resurrection."[266]

This Hadith is also established regarding the one who circulates lies and it is taken from him till it reaches distant areas.

Abu Hurayrah رضي الله عنه said, "Allah's Messenger ﷺ said, 'The signs of the hypocrite are three: when he talks, he lies, when he promises he fails, and when he is entrusted he betrays."[267]

264 Reported by Imam At-Tirmidhi in his *Sunan*: The Book on the Description of The Last Day: 4/668; and said about it: *HasanSahih*.

265 Reported by Imam Al-Bukhaari in his Sahih: The Book of Conduct: The Chapter on Allah's saying: **"O you who believe! Be afraid of Allah, and be with those who are true (in words and deeds)"** and What is Prohibited of Falsehood: 8/30.

266 Reported by Imam Al-Bukhaari in his *Sahih*: The Book on Funerals: 2/125-126.

267 Reported by Imam Al-Bukhaari in his *Sahih*: The Book of Conduct: The Chapter on Allah's saying: **"O you who believe! Be afraid of Allah, and be with those who are true (in words and deeds)"** and What is Prohibited of Falsehood: 8/30.

Bahz bin Hukaym from his father from his grand-father ﷺ said, "I heard Allah's Messenger ﷺ saying, 'Woe to the one who gives narration to amuse people and lies. Woe to him, woe to him!'"[268]

—Forms of Truthfulness

There are different forms of truthfulness:

1. Being truthful in speech

2. Being truthful in intents and desire which goes back to sincerity – and it has had been discussed.

3. Being truthful about determination to engage in goodness.

4. Being truthful in good deeds.

5. Being truthful in the realization of the ranks in the religion such as fear of Allah, hope, reverence, ascetism, pleasure (with the rulings of the religion) and reliance on Allah and loving Him and others.

—Some Stories of the Truthful

1. The story of Ka'b bin Maalik – which had been mentioned under repentance.

2. Rib'ee bin Haraash (d. 81 AH) – the great scholar of Hadith - had two male children disobedient to the ruler. So, an informant came to Al-Hajjaj and said, "'It is

268 Reported by Imam At-Tirmidhi in his *Sunan*: The Book on Ascetics: The Chapter on What is Reported about Whoever Says a Word to Amuse People: 4/557; and said: A *Hasan* Hadith

thought that Rib'ee bin Haraash will not lie but his two male children have violated the law." Al-Hajjaaj then sent for him. He asked him, "Where are your two children?" He answered, "They are both at home – And help is sought from Allah." Al-Hajjaaj then said, "They are both yours." Hajjaaj was impressed by his truthfulness.[269]

3. Abu 'Imran Az-Zujaajee said, "My mother died and I inherited a house which I sold for fifty *Deenaar*s. I set out for the pilgrimage and when I reached Abil, a robber came to me and said, 'What is with you?' I said to myself: 'Truthfulness is good', and then replied, 'Fifty *Deenaar*s.'

   Then he said: 'Give them to me.' I gave him the parcel and he counted it and it was fifty. Then he said to me, 'Take it, for your truthfulness has influenced me.' Then he descended his beast of burden and said to me, 'Ride on it.' I said: I do not want it but he insisted I must. He insisted again and so, I rode on it. He then said, 'I will take to your character.' When it reached the following year, he came to meet me and never left me until he died."[270]

12.2 *As-Sabr* (Patience)

It is from the most important Islamic characters and the most obligatory on the servant. It is to faith as the head to the body. Patience brings about all good but is from the most difficult affairs for the servant. No one attains patience except he to whom Allah grants protection and mercy.

Lexically, *Sabr* is: keeping back and refraining.

269 See: *Ithaaf Saadat il-Muttaqeen*: 13/135-158.
270 *Ithaaf Saadat il-Muttaqeen*: 13/161.

Technically, it is "keeping back the soul from apprehension and resentment, holding back the tongue from complains and refraining the limbs from evils."[271]

—Some Verses Regarding the Excellence of Patience

Allah the Mighty and Exalted said,

... وَتَمَّتْ كَلِمَتُ رَبِّكَ ٱلْحُسْنَىٰ عَلَىٰ بَنِيٓ إِسْرَٰٓءِيلَ بِمَا صَبَرُوا۟ ... ﴿١٣٧﴾

«And the fair Word of your Lord was fulfilled for the Children of Israel, because of their patience».

Al-A'raf (Q7:137)

He – Glorious is He – also said,

إِنَّمَا يُوَفَّى الصَّابِرُونَ أَجْرَهُمْ بِغَيْرِ حِسَابٍ

«Only those who are patient shall receive their rewards in full, without reckoning».

Az-Zumar (Q39:10)

Likewise, He said,

.... وَلَنَجْزِيَنَّ ٱلَّذِينَ صَبَرُوٓا۟ أَجْرَهُم بِأَحْسَنِ مَا كَانُوا۟ يَعْمَلُونَ ﴿٩٦﴾

«And those who are patient, We will certainly pay

271 See: *Tahdheeb Madaarij is-Saalikeen*: pg. 353.

them a reward in proportion to the best of what they used to do.»

An-Nahl (Q16:96)

Some Ahadith Regarding Patience

Suhayb Ar-Rumi رضي الله عنه said that Allah's Messenger ﷺ said, "Wondrous is the case of a believer; there is good in all of his affairs. And that is not for anyone but the believer. If he experiences joy, he gives thanks and that is good for him. If he experiences adversity, he is patient and that is good for him."[272]

Abu Maalik Al-Ash'aree رضي الله عنه said that Allah's Messenger ﷺ said, "Cleanliness is half of faith, (saying :) *Alhamdulillaah* (All praise is due to Allah) fills the scales, (saying :) *SubhaanAllah wal-Hamdulillaah* (Glorious is Allah and All praise is due to Allah) fills the space between the heavens and the earth. The prayer is light, charity is proof (of faith) and patience is a glow..."[273]

Abu Sa'eed Al-Khudree رضي الله عنه said, "He who seeks patience, Allah bestows steadfastness upon him. And no one is bestowed a favour better and more comprehensive like patience."[274]

Mahmood bin Labeed رضي الله عنه reported that Allah's Messenger ﷺ said,[275] "If Allah likes a people, He puts them to trial.

272 Reported by Imam Muslim in his *Sahih*: The Book on Ascetics: The Chapter on Different Narrations: 18/417.

273 Reported by Imam Muslim in his *Sahih*: The Book on Purification: Chapter on The Prayer is Light...:3/457.

274 Reported by Imam Al-Bukhaari in his *Sahih*: The Book on Zakaah: The Chapter on being Self-Sufficient away from Asking: 2/151-152.

275 The Hadith is *Sahih* (authentic). See: *At-Targeeb wat-Tarheeb* 3/1231 (Published by Maktabat ul-Ma'aarif, Riyadh) **(TN)**

So whoever is patient is bestowed patience and whoever is apprehensive gets apprehension."[276]

—Virtues and Meaning of Patience

- It is swallowing bitterness without frowning.
- It is said: getting the self used to the onslaught of dislikes.
- It is said: it is being steadfast with Allah and facing His trials with large-heartedness.
- Take to patience. If it kills you, you die a martyr and if it leaves you, you live with honour.
- Abu Dardaa ﷺ said, "The peak of faith is being patient with rulings and pleased with pre-ordainments."[277]
- Sufyaan bin 'Uyaynah (d. 198 AH) ﷺ said regarding His saying: *"And We made from among them (Children of Israel), leaders, giving guidance under Our Command, when they were patient"*: "They took to the most important matter and they were made the leaders"[278] that is; they took to patience which is the most important matter.

Patience over difficulties brings about benefits.[279]

Be patient, O wise servant

276 Imam Al-Mundhiree said in *At-Targeeb wat-Tarheeb* 4/283: Reported by Ahmad and its narrators are reliable.

277 *Ithaaf us-Saadat il-Muttaqeen*: 11/13.

278 *Tahdheeb Madaarij is-Saalikeen*: pg. 356.

279 *Nuzhat ul-Fudalaa*: 3/1363.

Perhaps, after your patience you will not be disappointed

And when every event ends

There is after it, a near relief.

Forms of Patience

There are different forms of patience:

1. Being patient about obedience to Allah the Mighty and Sublime.

2. Being patient away from disobedience to Allah – Glorious is He.

3. Being patient over trials.

The first and second forms are connected to the choice of the servant. As for the third form, the servant has no choice regarding it.[280]

From the best examples of being patient away from sin is that of Prophet Yusuf عليه السلام, "He was an unmarried young man, not having any substitute or what calms his desire. He was a stranger, and the stranger is usually not shy of what he is shy of while with his companions, those who know him and his household while in a strange land. He was a slave; and the slave – also – his restrain is not like that of the free-born. (On the other hand), the woman was beautiful, of high status and his female master. The supervisor was away. She was the one that invited him to herself and was the one so desirous of him. Even she threatened him with

280 *Tahdheeb Madaarij is-Saalikeen*: pg. 353.

imprisonment and disgrace if he refused. Despite all these insinuations, he was consciously patient out of preference for what is with Allah."[281]

Allah (the Exalted) commanded being patient. He said:

فَٱصْبِرْ صَبْرًا جَمِيلًا ۝٥

«So be patient (O Muhammad ﷺ), with a good patience».

Al-Ma'arij (Q70:5)

Here, good patience is that which is not accompanied by or include any complains.

—Some Points to Note

1. To lay complains to Allah (the Exalted) does not contradict patience:

Ya'qoob عليه السلام promised to be patient in a nice manner, and Allah – the most High – narrating his condition said:

.... قَالَ بَلْ سَوَّلَتْ لَكُمْ أَنفُسُكُمْ أَمْرًا ۖ فَصَبْرٌ جَمِيلٌ ۖ وَٱللَّهُ ٱلْمُسْتَعَانُ عَلَىٰ مَا تَصِفُونَ ۝١٨

«He said: 'Nay, but your ownselves have made up a tale. So (for me) patience is most fitting. And it is

281 The last reference.

Allah (Alone) Whose help can be sought against that which you assert.'»

Yusuf (Q12:18)

Despite that, he turned his complains to Allah (the Exalted):

قَالَ إِنَّمَآ أَشْكُواْ بَثِّي وَحُزْنِيٓ إِلَى ٱللَّهِ .... ﴿٨٦﴾

«I only complain of my grief and sorrow to Allah».

Yusuf (Q12:86)

Likewise Allah's Prophet, Ayub عليه السلام; Allah – the most High - said regarding him:

.... إِنَّا وَجَدْنَٰهُ صَابِرًاۚ نِّعْمَ ٱلْعَبْدُ إِنَّهُۥٓ أَوَّابٌ ﴿٤٤﴾

«Truly! We found him patient. How excellent (a) slave! Verily, he was ever oft-returning in repentance (to Us)!»

Saad (Q38:44)

He laid his complains to Allah (the Exalted) indirectly. He said,

.... أَنِّي مَسَّنِيَ ٱلضُّرُّ وَأَنتَ أَرْحَمُ ٱلرَّٰحِمِينَ ﴿٨٣﴾

«Verily, distress has seized me, and You are the Most Merciful of all those who show mercy.»

Al-Anbiyaa (Q21:83)

What contradicts patience is to complain about Allah and not complaining to Allah.[282]

When Hassan Al-Basree reads this verse: *"Truly! We found him patient…"*, he would cry and say: "How Wondrous is He, He gave and praised." That is, He is the Bestower of patience and the One praising (the patient) – Glorious is He.

2. **Being patient about acts of obedience is the greatest form of patience. The servant has three conditions regarding obedience:**

    i. The patience before the act of obedience; and that is by getting the intention right: being sincere.

    ii. The patience during the act of obedience so that one does not become neglectful of Allah while performing it or slacken from attaining its manners and rulings.

    iii. The patience after the act so that he does not render his deed vain or make himself vulnerable to show-off, popularity-seeking and being baffled at. Each of these things destroys actions. Allah (the Exalted) says:

.... وَلَا تُبْطِلُوٓا۟ أَعْمَٰلَكُمْ ﴿٣٣﴾

«And render not vain your deeds».

Muhammad (Q47:33)

282 *Tahdheeb Madaarij is-Saalikeen*: pg. 356 with slight modification and see: *Ithaaf usSadaat il-Muttaqeen*: 11/85.

3. Being patient during trial is at the first stroke

This is the praise-worthy patience during trial. Anas bin Maalik ﵁ said that Allah's Messenger ﷺ came to a woman who was wailing over (the death of) her child and said to her, "Fear Allah, and be patient." She retorted, "You do not care about my affliction." When he left, it was said to her that it was Allah's Messenger ﷺ. She regretted and went to his door but did not find gate-keepers (as is the manner of kings and rulers). So, she said, 'O Allah's Messenger, I did not recognize you.' He then remarked, "Patience is only at the first stroke" or he said, "During the first stroke."[283]

12.3 *At-Tawaadu'* (Humility)

It is the character of the believers, no one amongst them demonstrated it except that Allah increased him in rank and honour and exalt his mention amongst the people. Also no one amongst the Muslims abandons it except that he is afflicted with humiliation, made to be hated and disliked by the people, disliked and abandoned.

Fudayl bin 'Iyyaad ﵀ was asked about humility and he said, "(The humble) succumbs to the truth, complies with it and takes it from whoever says it."

It is said that, "It (i.e. humility) is lowering the wings and being flexible.[284]

On the other hand the arrogant is denied the favour of Allah the Mighty and Sublime and His gifts. Allah – Glorious is He – said,

283 Reported by Imam Muslim in his *Sahih*: The Book on Funerals: The Chapter on Patience is at the First Stroke: 6/525.

284 See: *Tahdheeb Madaarij is-Saalikeen*: pg. 429.

سَأَصۡرِفُ عَنۡ ءَايَٰتِيَ ٱلَّذِينَ يَتَكَبَّرُونَ فِي ٱلۡأَرۡضِ بِغَيۡرِ ٱلۡحَقِّ ... ﴿١٤٦﴾

«I shall turn away from My *Ayaat* (verses of the Qur'aan) those who behave arrogantly on the earth, without a right.»

Al-A'raf (Q7:146)

He – Glorious is He – also said,

.... كَذَٰلِكَ يَطۡبَعُ ٱللَّهُ عَلَىٰ كُلِّ قَلۡبِ مُتَكَبِّرٖ جَبَّارٖ ﴿٣٥﴾

«Thus does Allah seal up the heart of every arrogant, tyrant. (So they cannot guide themselves to the Right Path)».

Ghafir (Q40:35)

Virtues of Humility and Abhorrence of Arrogance

1. 'Iyyaad bin Hammaar ﷺ who said: Allah's Messenger ﷺ said: "Allah inspired me (to say to you) that you should be humble such that no one will pride himself over anyone and no one will oppress anyone."[285]

2. Abu Hurayrah ﷺ reported that Allah's Messenger ﷺ said, "No charity reduces anything from a wealth (since it actually brings Allah's blessings to it). Allah increases a servant in honour whenever he pardons, and no one

285 Reported by Imam Muslim in his *Sahih*: The Book on Paradise and the Description of Its Enjoyment: The Chapter on the Attributes of the People of Paradise and the People of the Hell: 18/323

is humble for Allah's sake except that Allah raises his rank."[286]

3. Abu Sa'eed Al-Khudree and Abu Hurayrah ﷺ both said that Allah's Messenger ﷺ said, "Allah the Mighty and Sublime says, 'Glory is my covering and pride is my cloak. Whoever contends with me I punish him.'"[287]

4. Abu Salamah bin Abdir-Rahman bin 'Awf who said, Abdullah bin Umar and Abdullah bin 'Amr bin Al-'Aas ﷺ both met at Marwa and discussed. Then, Abdullah bin 'Amr left and Abdullah bin Umar remained and started weeping. A man asked him, 'What makes you cry, O Abu Abdir-Rahmaan?' He answered, 'This (i.e. Abdullah bin 'Amr) said he heard Allah's Messenger ﷺ saying, 'Whoever has pride equal to the weight of a grain of mustard seed in his heart, Allah will turn him down on his faces in the Fire.'"[288]

5. Abu Hurayrah ﷺ that Allah's Messenger ﷺ said, "While a man walked dressed in *Hulla*,[289] he was impressed by himself, with well combed hairs, moving in a lofty proud manner. Suddenly, Allah caused the earth to swallow him up. He will continue to sink in it till the Day of Ressurrection."[290]

---

286 Reported by Imam Muslim in his *Sahih*: The Book on Benevolence, Relationship and Etiquettes: The Chapter on Pardoning and Humility: 16/109.

287 Reported by Imam Muslim in his *Sahih*: The Book on Benevolence, Relationship and Etiquettes: The Chapter on The prohibition of Arrogance.

288 Haafidh Al-Mundhiree said: Reported by Ahmad, and its narrators are reporters of authentic narrations: See: *At-Targeeb wat-Tarheeb*: 3/566, and likewise Imam Al-Haythamee, he said in *Majmau' Az-Zawaaid*: 1/103.

289 "Two pieces of cloth worn such that one above the other." Fath ul-Baaree: ...

290 Reported by Al-Bukhaari in his *Sahih*: The Book on Dressing: The Chapter on Whoever Drags his cloth Out of Pride: 6/183.

6. Ibn Umar ﷺ said, I heard Allah's Messenger ﷺ saying: "Whoever feels proud or walks in a lofty proud manner, he will meet Allah (the Exalted) while He is angry with him."[291]

7. Our Prophet ﷺ was the most humble of people and the farthest away from arrogance. Abu Hurayrah ﷺ reported that, "Jibreel sat with the Prophet ﷺ and looked at the heaven and there was an angel. Jibreel said, 'This is an angel; it has not descended since it was created and before the Hour.' When it descended, it said, 'O Muhammad, my Lord has sent me to you (asking), 'Should I make you a king and a prophet or a servant and Messenger?' Jibreel said, 'Be humble to your Lord, O Muhammad.' He ﷺ said, 'Rather, a servant and Messenger."[292]

Ibn Abbas ﷺ said that the Prophet ﷺ would sit on the floor, fetter sheep and attend to the invitation of a slave (for food) where wheat bread is served.[293]

The pious predecessors loved humility and warned against arrogance. Yusuf bin Asbaat, the ascetic, said, "Some devoutness with humility is more beneficial than much effort on deeds." He also said: "The peak of humility is that you do not meet anyone except that you find yourself obligated to him."[294]

Imam Ash-Shafi'i said: "Humility is from the noble

291 Imam Al-Haythamee said in *Majma' uz-Zawaaid*: 1/103: "Reported by Ahmad and its narrators are those of authentic narrations".

292 Imam Al-Haythamee said in *Majma' uz-Zawaaid*: 9/22 that the Hadith is reported by Ahmad and its narrators are those of authentic narrations.

293 Imam Al-Haythamee said in *Majma' uz-Zawaaid*: 9/23: reported by At-Tabaraanee and its chain is *Hasan* (good).

294 Reported by Imam At-Tirmidhi: The Book on Benevolence, Relationship and Etiquettes: Chapter on What is reported on Arrogance; and At-Tirmidhi said: This is a *HasanSahih* Hadith.

characters and arrogance is from the traits of the ignoble. Humility brings about love and contentment brings about rest." He also said: "The highest in rank amongst the people is the one who sees not his rank and the most honourable of them is the one who does not see his honour."[295]

Two Points of Note

The First: It is not the love for good wears or food, and the love for good things and enjoying the things of this world – to an extent – that is considered arrogance. Abdullah bin Mas'ood رضي الله عنه reported from the Prophet ﷺ who said, "The one who has an atom weight of arrogance in his heart will not enter Paradise, and the one with an atom weight of faith in his heart will not enter the Fire." He (Ibn Mas'ood) said, "A man then asked him, 'I like my clothes and shoes to be nice?'" He ﷺ said: "Allah is beautiful, He likes beauty; but arrogance is denying truth and looking down upon people".[296]

Imam At-Tirmidhi رحمه الله said, "The people of knowledge have said regarding the explanation of this Hadith that: the one with an atom weight of faith in his heart will not enter the Fire means that he will not be in it forever. A similar report from Abu Sa'eed Al-Khudree رضي الله عنه from the Prophet ﷺ says, 'Whoever has an atom weight of faith in his heart will be taken out of the Fire.' Many of the *Taabi'een* explain this verse:

295 That is: he does not consider his rank and honour a reason to look down upon the people. **(TN)**

296 Reported by Imam At-Tirmidhi: The Book on Benevolence, Relationship and Etiquettes: The Chapter on What is reported on Arrogance; and At-Tirmidhi said; this is a *Hasan Sahih* Hadith.

رَبَّنَآ إِنَّكَ مَن تُدْخِلِ ٱلنَّارَ فَقَدْ أَخْزَيْتَهُۥ ... ﴿١٩٢﴾

«Our Lord! Verily, whom You admit to the Fire, indeed, You have disgraced him»,

Aal Imran (Q3:192)

They say, 'Whoever stays in the Hell forever, you have disgraced him,'"

The Other: The believing slave should avoid pride and (be careful about) what brings about it such as:

1. Knowledge.
2. Acting upon good deeds.
3. Lineage.
4. Beauty.
5. Power.
6. Wealth.
7. Much of helpers.[297]

These seven attributes are praise-worthy in themselves but could lead to arrogance. Thus, the pious servant should not be deceived by any of that leading him to become proud and haughty – And Allah is the Source of help.

297 For further explanations on this matter, see: *Ithaaf us-Saadat il-Muttaqeen*: 1/286 and what comes after it.

Chapter 13

Encouragement upon Good Characters and Warning against Ignoble Conduct

1. Abu Hurayrah ﵁ said that Allah's Messenger ﷺ said, "Beware of suppositions, for supposition is the most false of words (that the mind tells). Do not spy at one another, do not envy one another, do not abandon one another, and do not hate one another. Be you all servants of Allah, as brothers."[298]

2. 'Imran bin Husayn ﵁ said that Allah's Messenger ﷺ said, "Bashfulness brings not but good."[299]

3. Jaabir bin Abdillaah Al-Bajalee reported from the Prophet ﷺ that, "Whoever does not show mercy will not receive mercy."[300]

4. Nu'maan bin Basheer ﵁ said that Allah's Messenger ﷺ said, "You will find the believers in their mutual show of

---

298 Reported by imam Al-Bukhaari in his *Sahih*: The Book on Manners: The Chapter on What is Prohibited of Envying and Abandoning One Another: 8/23.

299 The last reference: The Book on Bashfulness: 8/11.

300 The last reference: The Chapter on Mercy to the People and the Beasts; 8/11.

mercy, love, and compassion like the body (with respect to its limbs); when a limb suffers, the rest of the body calls in each other for it with sleeplessness and fever."[301]

5. Abu Shurayh Al-'Adawee ﵁ said, "My ears heard and my eyes saw when the Prophet ﷺ spoke and said, "Whoever believes in Allah and the Last Day should honour his neighbor; and whoever believes in Allah and the Last Day should honour his guest to his allowable (time)." He asked, "What is his allowable (time), O Messenger of Allah?" He replied, "A day and night. The entertainment is for three days; so whatever comes after that is charity to him. And whoever believes in Allah and the Last Day should say a nice word or remain silent."[302]

6. Abu Ayub Al-Ansari ﵁ said that Allah's Messenger ﷺ said, "It is not right for the Muslim to abandon his brother for more than three days such that they would meet and this will turn away and that will turn away. And the best of them both is the one that commenced greeting with *Salam*."[303]

7. Ibn Umar ﵄ reported that Allah's Messenger ﷺ said, "A Muslim is the brother of another Muslim; he will not be unjust to him and will not expose him to harm. Whoever attends to the need of his brother, Allah fulfills his needs. Whoever removes a distress from a Muslim, Allah will remove a distress for him by it on the Day of Judgment. Whoever covers (the fault) a Muslim, Allah

---

301 The last reference: 12/8.

302 The last reference: 8/35.

303 Reported by Imam Muslim in his *Sahih*: The Book on Benevolence, Relationship and Etiquettes: The Chapter on Finding out About Abandoning for More Than Three days without a Legal Reason: 16/91.

will cover him (his faults) on the Day of Judgment."[304]

8. Abu Hurayrah رضي الله عنه narrated that Allah's Messenger ﷺ said, "Do you know who is broke?" They answered, "The person who is broke amongst us is the one without a Dirham or any belongings." So, he explained, "The person who is really broke in my *Ummah* is the one who will come on the Day of Judgment with the prayer, fasting and charity. He will come having abused this, slandered that, consumed the wealth of this (illegally), spilled the blood of this and beaten this. So, this will be given from his good deeds, that from it and when his good deeds are exhausted before he settles what is against him, it will be taken from their sins and thrown at him and then, he will be thrown in the Fire."[305]

9. Abu Hurayrah رضي الله عنه said that Allah's Messenger ﷺ said, "Do you know what is back-biting?" They replied, "Allah and His Messenger know best." He ﷺ explained, "Saying about your brother, what he dislikes." It was said, "What if what I say of my brother is right?" He ﷺ said, "If what you say about him is right of him, then you have backbitten him. But if it is not of him, you have slandered him."[306]

10. Jareer bin Abdillaah Al-Bajalee رضي الله عنه said, "Allah's Messenger ﷺ said, 'Whoever is denied gentleness is denied goodness.'"[307]

11. Abu Dardaa رضي الله عنه said, "Allah's Messenger ﷺ said, 'Those

---

304 The last reference: The Chapter of The Prohibition of Injustice: 16/104.
305 Reported by Imam Muslim in his *Sahih*: The Chapter on The Prohibition of Oppression: 16/105.
306 The last reference: The Chapter on The Prohibition of Backbiting: 16/110.
307 The last reference: The Chapter on the Excellence of Gentleness: 16/112.

who curse frequently will not be intercessors or witnesses (against past nations) on the Day of Judgment.'"[308]

12. Abu Hurayrah ﵁ reported that the Prophet ﷺ said, "The one who throws the people is not (necessarily) the strong but the strong one is he who controls himself during anger."[309]

13. Abu Hurayrah ﵁ narrated that the Prophet ﷺ said, "I saw a man enjoying the bounties of Paradise for a tree he cut from the road because it was harming the people."[310]

14. Abu Hurayrah ﵁ said, "The Prophet ﷺ said, 'Do not despise any good deed even if it is meeting your brother with a cheerful face.'"[311]

Allah – knows Best and is the most Just. May the peace and blessings of Allah be upon our leader, Muhammad, his household and his entire companions.

All praise is due to Allah, the Lord of all that exists.

308 The last reference: The Chapter on Cursing Beasts and Others.
309 Reported by Imam Muslim: The Chapter on the one who Controls Himself during Anger: 16/125.
310 The last reference: The Virtue of Removing Harm from the Road: 16/131.
311 The last reference: Chapter on the Excellence of Cheerful Looks and Interceding Regarding What does not include a Prohibition: 16/136.